Making Meaning

MW01613426

A Guide for Passing the Regents' Essay

SECOND EDITION

Sarah L. Larson
DeKalb College, North

KENDALL/HUNT PUBLISHING COMPANY
4050 Westmark Drive   Dubuque, Iowa 52002

Illustrations by Walt Griffin

Copyright © 1990, 1993 by Sarah L. Larson

ISBN 0-7872-0621-0

Printed in the United States of America

10 9 8 7 6 5 4 3 2

CONTENTS

Preface **vii**

PART I: An Overview of the Regents' Test   **1**

Questions and Answers About the Reading and Writing Exam   **1**

PART II: The Regents' Test Preparation Seminar   **7**

The Regents' Test Preparation Seminar Outline   **8**
Commentary on the Regents' Test Handout   **9**
Application to Classroom Teaching   **12**
Rules for Panel Discussion   **14**
Discussion Evaluation Blank   **15**

PART III: The Regents' Test Preparation Seminar Handout   **17**

Instructions for Scoring Regents' Testing Program Essays   **18**
Questions and Answers on the Rating of Regents' Test Essays   **22**
Guidelines for Writing the Regents' Essay   **26**
Analysis of Regents' Essay/Content/Form/Mechanics   **27**
An Example of What You Do Not Want to Write   **28**
Regents' Essay Checklist   **29**
Analysis of Formulaic Failing Essay   **30**
Essays Illustrating "Although Clause"   **31**
Diagrams of Strategies for Composing
   the Regents' Essay and References to Models and Analyses   **34**
USA Today as a Teaching Tool   **37**
Regents' Testing Program Essay Booklet   **39**
Worksheet on Regents' Examination Topics   **43**
The Expository Essay with Clustering of Major Topics   **44**

PART IV: Analyses of Regent's Essays   **45**

The Formulaic Approach   **46**
The Structured Opening Options   **47**
The Two Part Thesis with a Subdivision   **50**
The Humorous/Satirical Development   **52**
The Contrastive Paragraph or "Although Clause Strategy"   **53**
The Narrative Option   **55**
The Descriptive Strategy   **57**

PART V: Alternate Approaches in Composition   **59**

    The Narrative Approach   **60**
      Definition of the Narrative Essay   **60**
      Six Points for Success   **60**
      Regents' Essays Developed by Narration   **61**
      Narrative Introductions   **65**
      Extended Examples   **66**
    The Descriptive Approach   **69**
      Definition of the Descriptive Essay   **69**
      Topics Inviting Descriptive Development   **70**
      Regents' Essays Developed by Description   **71**
      Descriptive Introduction   **74**
    The Argumentative Approach   **77**
      Definition of the Argumentative Essay   **77**
      Outline of "Although Clause" Structure   **78**
      Regents' Essays Developed by the "Although Clause" Approach   **78**
      Clustering of Controversial Issues   **81**
      Exercises for Clusters of Argumentative Topics   **82**
      The Clusters   **82**
    The Expository Approach   **85**
      Definition of the Expository Essay   **85**
      Discussion Topics Based on the Major Clusters   **86**
      Optional: Plan for Formal Discussion, Composition, and Checklist   **87**
      Application of Plan   **87**
      Essay Resulting from the Application of the Plan   **88**
    Advantages of Alternate Approaches   **90**
    Practice with Paired Topics   **90**
    Final Approaches   **95**
      Saving Your Essays   **95**
      Preparing for the Test Date   **96**
        Physical Preparation   **96**
        Mental Preparation   **96**

PART VI: RTP—A Personalized Approach to Grammar   **99**

    Writing and Proofing Your Essay   **100**
    Definition of Errors   **102**
    Spelling   **103**
      Personal Spelling List   **103**
      Using the Dictionary   **103**
      Visual Spelling   **104**
      Finger Spelling   **105**
      Memory Aids   **105**
      Regular Patterns   **105**
      Spelling Rules   **106**
      Words That Sound Alike   **108**
      Exercises on "Sound Alikes"   **109**

The Big Four   **110**

  Eliminating Fragments   **111**

    The Fragment Without a Subject   **111**

    The Fragment Without a Complete Verb   **111**

    The Fragment Without Subject or Verb   **112**

    The Fragment Without "Independence"   **112**

  Eliminating Comma Splices and Run-ons   **113**

    Graphic Summary of Punctuation   **114**

    Conjunctive Adverbs and Transitional Expressions   **114**

  Three Suggestions for Eliminating Frag/CS/RO   **115**

  Exercises for Frag/CS/RO Identification   **116**

  Eliminating Errors in Subject/Verb Agreement   **118**

    The Major Rule   **118**

    Twelve Rules to Follow   **118**

    Helpful Reminders   **120**

    Exercises in Subject-Verb Agreement   **120**

PART VII: Appendix   **123**

Approved Regents' Test Essay Topics   **123**

PREFACE

Our nation is worried about its schools and the ability of its students not only to assume leadership positions in our country but also to compete internationally. And such concern is warranted since the United States is currently ranked tenth of the top ten industrialized nations in all academic disciplines. Where does the responsibility for such disappointing results lie? The schools point their collective finger at the fragmentation of the American family. The parents blame the educators for their emphasis on personal growth rather than on basic skills. The students are caught in the middle with the feeling that they have become cogs in a wheel that is frantically spinning but getting nowhere.

In the meantime, the national government has relinquished to the states much of the power to deal with the educational crisis but has given them little guidance and even less financial support. In the midst of all this turmoil, the University System of Georgia has emerged as a leader in certifying that its graduates have adequate reading and writing skills. Such efforts are praiseworthy, for when the students in the state college and university system are aware of what is expected of them, they are able to take charge of their learning and achieve a certain pride in meeting the challenge. It is our duty as educators to fully inform them of the assessment process, to make the testing as fair and democratic as possible, and to provide the opportunity for appeal if a discrepancy occurs in the rating process.

Making Meaning is an effort to make public the issue of literacy testing in the Regents' System, and at the same time to give its students all the tools needed to empower them to pass the essay test. The book also contains information on how to set up a Regents' Test Preparation Seminar and a hand-out with commentary preceding it to prepare instructors to conduct such a session. I am grateful to my colleagues at DeKalb College who field tested the pilot project—particularly Joanne Burgess, who gave me support to complete the text. A thank you also goes to my students who gave me suggestions on what worked and didn't work in the RTP process. And finally, I wish to thank my long suffering family who think that a home-cooked meal is a vision to behold.

Sarah L. Larson

PART I

AN OVERVIEW OF THE REGENTS' TEST

QUESTIONS AND ANSWERS ABOUT THE READING AND WRITING EXAM

Why is there a Regents' Test?

The Board of Regents, which sets policies for the University System of Georgia, instituted the Regents' Exam so that each college and university in that system could "assure the other institutions and the system as a whole, that students obtaining a degree from that institution possess certain minimal skills of reading and writing" (Regents' Policy Statement).

When should I take the Regents' Test?

Students should take the Regents' Test after completing the required basic English courses with a "C" or better or after completing 45 hours of collegiate level coursework. However, statistics indicate that students have a higher pass rate if they take the test the quarter following the successful completion of their first collegiate level English composition course.

When must I take the test?

The Regents' Test must be taken during the quarter of enrollment immediately following the completion of 60 college-level quarter credit hours regardless of whether the student has taken or passed specific courses, including English courses.

Where do I register for the test?

Students must be currently enrolled to take the Regents' Test which is given before midterm each quarter. At most Regents' institutions, eligible students sign up to take the test at registration or early in the quarter so that the testing office can order the required number of test booklets.

What if I am a student from a Regents' institution and wish to take the test at another System college or university?

Students who attend other Georgia University System institutions can register to take the Regents' Test at member institutions only if they have a letter in advance

1

from the Regents' Testing Coordinator at their school giving them permission to take the test at a designated institution in the University System of Georgia.

How important is the Exam?

Students cannot receive associate or baccalaureate degrees from the University System of Georgia until they pass the Regents' Test. All Regents' schools provide preparation courses to help students fulfill the requirement.

What is the Pass Rate on the Exam?

The Regents' Testing Program office releases quarterly statistics indicating that approximately 65–67 percent of all students who take the exam for the first time pass it and that 45 percent who repeat the exam have passing grades.

What happens if I fail one or both parts of the Exam?

A student who does not pass both parts may retake all or the part he/she failed a second time before being required to take remediation if the student has not accumulated 75 hours.

When must I take a reading or essay preparation course?

Each Regents' institution can set more stringent requirements for enrolling in preparation courses, but all System colleges and universities require students who have completed 75 hours and who have not passed the test to take remediation classes until they pass the test.

Does everyone have to take the Test?

Students enrolled in any Georgia University System college or university must take and pass the test as a requirement for receiving an A.A., an A.S. degree (associate degree), or a baccalaureate degree. STUDENTS ENROLLED IN A.A.S. DEGREE PROGRAMS COMMONLY REFERRED TO AS CAREER PROGRAMS ARE NOT REQUIRED TO PASS THE REGENTS' TEST. However, System institutions may elect to require the test for those degrees. In addition, students holding baccalaureate or higher degrees from an accredited institutuion of higher education will not be required to complete the Regents' test in order to receive a degree from a University System institution.

What if my first language is not English?

Regents' Policy states that "students whose mother tongue is other than English may be exempted by the institution provided appropriate local procedures are employed to certify the competence of those students earning a degree." Each institution sets up criteria to satisfy competency requirements. Find out what your institution requires.

What if I am a handicapped student?

"For extraordinary situations, each institution will develop special procedures for certifying the competence of students" (Regents' Policy Statement). As a result of this Policy, each institution assesses student handicaps and may set up alternate measures for certifying competency. Students should contact their test coordinator for guidance in this area.

What kind of test is the Regents' Test?

The Regents' Test has two sections, essay and reading, administered in that order. The essay section requires students to write an essay on one of the two topics given. During the final 15 minutes of the essay portion of the Regents' Test, students will be permitted to use a dictionary. They must bring their own dictionary and are not permitted to share it. The timed reading test includes word usage and reading comprehension.

How long is the test?

The test lasts two hours—60 minutes for the essay and 60 minutes for the reading. But students should also expect to add on 30 minutes of preparation time to check in and to fill in the answer sheets. The class schedule each quarter lists the date, time, and place of the test, which is administered at a variety of times and locations for the students' convenience.

What should I bring with me?

The students should bring two number two pencils for the information sheet and for the reading exam and two pens—either blue or black—in case one runs out of ink—for the essay component. The essay will not be rated if it is written in pencil but erasable pen may be used. Other stipulations are that red, peacock blue, or green ink cannot be used, and neither can white liquid ink. As stated before, students may bring a dictionary to use during the last 15 minutes of the essay exam but may not share it with another student.

When will I know if I passed the test?

The scores are returned to the colleges before the end of the quarter and entered on the students' grade reports. As indicated earlier, if the student passes only one part of the test, that partial pass is recorded, and only the remaining part needs to be taken to meet graduation requirements.

How can I prepare for the test?

Practicing the test in simulated test conditions is a good way to prepare for the timed essay portion and reading test. Each college gives Regents' Test Preparation Seminars to inform students about the test and to hand out material to aid them. The writing and reading labs assist students who wish to practice for the test or to have their essays evaluated. Reading a daily newspaper or weekly news magazine will help students be aware of the numerous social, economic, and political issues addressed in the 493 published essay topics. <u>The Polishing Cloth</u>, a DeKalb College magazine of student writing, publishes practice Regents' essays and actual Regents' essays which have received an above average rating. This publication which can be purchased in all campus bookstores helps students see how fellow students have developed a number of the 493 published topics and what standards are employed. When taking the reading test, students should try to answer all the questions since they are not penalized for wrong answers. Locating the test site early to avoid last minute frustration, practicing relaxation exercises, taking the test seriously but knowing that the majority pass the first time—all these tips should contribute to a positive approach to taking the test. Finally, student writers will benefit from knowing themselves well, being good observers, keeping abreast of community lore and world events, and realizing that they have something important to say.

<u>What kinds of topics are printed on the essay test booklets?</u>

Two types of topics are used—one within the students' life experience and one outside, requiring knowledge of history, literature, or socio-economic-political issues. Students have the choice between the two and should write on the topic they know most about, because no extra credit is given for selecting the more difficult, abstract, or philosophical topic. Brainstorming or jotting down ideas about the topic on the space provided on the front of the booklet will help students decide on the strongest topic for them. The very act of writing down thoughts related to the topic helps students construct a thesis and find supporting details. Since the 493 topics are published, clustering the topics seems to be a helpful way to inform students about the major categories included. More than <u>fifty each</u> focus on "What's Happening to the American Family?," "Growing Old in America," "Crime—Cause or Prevention," "The Quality of Television," and "Health and Physical Fitness." <u>Thirty or fewer</u> center around each of the following: "The Economic State of the Nation," "America's Role in the Free World," and "National Defense." By far the <u>largest group</u> of topics (over 65) concerns "U.S. Public School Education—Strengths and Weaknesses." Since a large number of paired topics are used for each testing session, students should not expect those sitting near them to have the same set of topics.

<u>What are the standards used in grading the essay?</u>

The Regents' testing office suggests that "in general, the pass rating will require that you (1) state and develop a central idea; (2) have an organization which is indicative of an overall plan; (3) deal with the assigned topic; and (4) avoid serious errors in diction, sentence structure, and paragraph development." The organization and the content are the most important factors in determining a passing essay, but students must be aware that excessive, distracting errors will fail an essay. They should proof the test to avoid the major errors: the comma splice, the run-on, the fragment, and the subject-verb agreement errors.

<u>What is the procedure for grading the essays?</u>

All essays throughout the state are sent to a central office where they are mixed thoroughly and then sent to six or seven grading centers. The essays are rated holistically by three raters who are experienced composition instructors in the

University System. The graders do not know who wrote the essays or what school they come from. Since no marks are made on the paper and the rating is concealed, each grader assesses the composition with no knowledge of previous or subsequent evaluations. Raters record a social security number and a mark of (1) failing, (2) minimum pass, (3) above average, or (4) superior on a data processing sheet, and then a computer tabulates the results. Two of the three graders must have awarded the paper a (2) or higher in order for the student to receive a passing mark.

Can students see their tests after they turn them in?

Although the student is not allowed to see the actual reading test but only the score recording the correct number of answers on the print-out provided each Regents' institution, essays are returned to each campus to be reviewed by students who request to see them. Students should expect to see no marks on the booklet other than the raters' initials. The essay tests are stored in the writing lab at some colleges and or in the English departments or counseling centers at others. If the student passes the essay, he receives a "2," "3," or "4" mark beside his/her name and social security number on the print-out, but if the essay fails (1), all three ratings are revealed in a separate section of the data. This complete report allows the students to find out if they received one passing mark out of the three, allowing them to appeal the grade. Reading scores cannot be appealed and are determined by the number of correct answers, a score of 61 needed for passing.

What is the procedure for appealing the essay grade?

In November 1979, the Board of Regents adopted a policy that permits a formal review of the students' essays if they received at least one passing score among the three scores awarded.

The review procedures are as follows:

1. The student will initiate the on-campus review by contacting the testing coordinator. Although the procedures differ at System institutions, all require that the essay be appealed by mid-term in the quarter following the quarter when the test was taken. For example, an essay written in fall quarter must be appealed by midterm winter quarter or the student loses the opportunity for review.

2. The on-campus review committee consisting of three faculty members will re-score the essay, simulating the procedure used in the original evaluation. Therefore, the essay must receive two passing ratings of 2 or better to receive further consideration. The student will be notified concerning the results of the on-campus review.

3. If the on-campus panel recommends re-scoring of the essay, it will be sent along with comments of justification from the raters to the office of the System Director of the Regents' Testing Program.

4. The Director will utilize the services of three (3) experienced Regents' Essay scorers other than those involved in the original scoring of the essay to review the essay, following normal scoring procedures for the essay component of the

Regents' Test. The decision of the panel on the merits of the essay will be final. The student will be notified through the institution about the results of the review. The decision will be made before the Regents' Test is given mid-quarter.

PART II

THE REGENTS' TEST PREPARATION SEMINAR

Regents' Test Preparation Seminars are held each quarter approximately two weeks before the scheduled Regents' Test to help students mentally and emotionally prepare to take the system-wide test.

An overview of the test is given, and then the group is divided into two or three subgroups, depending on the number attending. Each subgroup rotates and receives information on the reading and essay tests and the writing lab. Strategies for passing the reading test and a sample test are included in the reading session. A similar workshop is held to prepare students for the essay test, accompanied by a handout and a brainstorming period on thesis construction. A visit to the writing lab to acquaint students with its services completes the workshop. Students are informed that their RTP essays are filed in the writing lab or counseling center and that they can make an appointment to review them. Many institutions have a follow-up session later in the week to give the students the opportunity to write a practice Regents' test essay in the actual auditorium (or classroom) where the test is administered. Those participating receive the actual Regents' topics in a simulated booklet and are instructed to write one hour, with the option of using their individual dictionaries or spellers during the last fifteen minutes. Those essays are read and rated by three graders, using the four point scale outlined by the University System Academic Committee on English. These mock Regents' essay tests are placed in the writing lab for students to review with the guidance of a tutor.

Students should take advantage of these quarterly workshops which thoroughly prepare them for the actual Regents' test mid-quarter.

THE REGENTS' TEST PREPARATION SEMINAR OUTLINE

The essay preparation handout provided for the students during the RTP Seminar may include the following:

1. "Instructions for Scoring Regents' Testing Program Essays" booklet (pp. 18–25)

2. Handouts from Georgia State University Writing Lab (pp. 26–28)

3. Regents' Essay Checklist (p. 29)

4. Sample student essays, illustrating the "although clause options" (pp. 31–33)

5. Diagrams of Strategies for Composing the Essay and references to models and detailed analyses. Options for introductions. Use of <u>USA Today</u> (pp. 34–37)

6. Regents' Essay Booklet (simulated) (pp. 39–42)

7. Exercise on Developing a Thesis—with emphasis on the "although clause" (p. 43)

8. Definition of Expository Essay with Clustering of Major Topics (p. 44)

WRITE ABOUT SOMETHING YOU DO OR SOMETHING YOU KNOW ABOUT.

WRITING CAN EXPRESS AN IDEA AND/OR AN EMOTION; IT EXPRESSES YOU.

COMMENTARY ON THE REGENTS' TEST PREPARATION SEMINAR HANDOUT

1. "Instructions for Scoring Regents' Testing Program Essays" booklet (pp. 18–25).

Approximately two weeks after the Regents' essays have been written, they are scored by Regents' System teachers of composition. In order to assure uniformity in the grading procedure these explicit "Instructions" are sent in advance to each volunteer grader. These instruction booklets describe the method of holistic grading and define the ratings assigned: (1), (2), (3), (4). Models are provided along with a thorough analysis of each essay. Questions and answers about essay rating further explain the procedure. This instruction booklet for raters is included to allow students to have valuable information about the scoring of their essays.

In addition to the "Instructions for Scoring Regents' Testing Program Essays" sent to each rater, a training workshop is held prior to the grading session. Copies of student essays are provided, and all instructors score the compositions and discuss their ratings. To further assure uniformity in grading, all raters receive a report of their scores to reveal their agreement with other graders in the system. Regents' raters take their job very seriously.

Readers of the scoring booklet need to be reminded that it is written with the English professor in mind. When the question is asked, "Must the essay have a thesis sentence to pass?" (p. 23), and the answer is "not necessarily" (p. 23), that response is written so the grader will not overlook a sophisticated essay with an implied thesis. The average essayist must realize that Georgia State University's research recorded in the handout (p. 27) reveals how important the thesis is to passing the essay exam—a three-star emphasis.

In response to question 7 in the raters' instructions about the use of statistics (p. 24), writers need help in collecting statistics they can easily use in the major clusterings of the 493 topics. Since most of the topics listed are on education (p. 44), students should be aware that knowing that the United States ranks tenth in education among the top ten industrialized nations and that one-third of our population is functionally illiterate adds depth and quality to their essays. The next largest clustering is "Crime—Cause or Prevention" and "What's Happening to the American Family?" (p. 44). Those writers that note that crime has tripled in the last decade, that more than 60% of crimes are drug related, or that the average number of years a murderer is incarcerated in Georgia is seven years are able to add significant, verifiable statistics to their Regents' exams. The topics related to the family are often embellished with the facts that over half the marriages in the United States end in divorce, that in the 1990's women will exceed the number of men in the workforce, that one out of four children lives in poverty and that the poverty is "pink," referring to women as single heads of households.

A Regents' topic on television provides information on another large clustering of 50–55 topics on "The Quality of Television" (p. 44): "According to studies, the average American watches television as much as six hours a day. Why do Americans watch so much television?" (p. 132). Other information helpful in writing on the TV topics include the influence of the Nielsen ratings of network programming to such an extent that the highly rated Home Improvement can garner $400,000 for a 30-second commercial. In addition, being aware of the graying of the United States will aid the composers of the 45–50 topics on "Growing Old in America." Although growing old in America is depressing compared to aging in the Far East where the elderly are respected and even worshipped, the increased political clout wielded by the older citizens will translate into better conditions for elders in the future.

The next large category of "Health and Physical Fitness" includes a number of newly added topics on the AIDS crisis that affects education and dating habits. Certainly helpful in topics related to "The Economic State of the Nation" is the knowledge that America is the biggest debtor nation and that the average U.S. citizen saves two percent of his salary while a Japanese worker saves twenty percent. Gathering statistics and detailed information on the major groups of topics not only makes the essay more interesting but also enhances the chances of passing the writing test.

2. Handouts from Georgia State University Writing Lab (pp. 26–28) Checklist (p. 27). This checklist from Georgia State University is based on research on the Regents' essay. Students should realize the importance of the asterisks placed by items of content, organization, and mechanics.

3. Regents' Essay Checklist (p. 29). In his recent book <u>Research on Composition</u>, George Hillocks, Jr. stresses the value of having a checklist for composition. In terms of improving the quality of writing, having the students apply "scales, criteria and specific questions . . . to their own and others' writing is two times more effective than free writing techniques" (249) states Hillocks. The checklist can also aid in collaborative learning in composition classes.

4. Sample student essays, illustrating the "although clause option" (pp. 31–33). One of the most important aspects of the seminar is the review of the thesis or main idea which controls the essay, the need for sharp divisions of the topic, the five paragraph essay which facilitates an organized approach to the topic, several types of introductions, and, most important of all, <u>alternate ways</u> to approach the formulaic three part thesis that enhance a student's control over the topic. The students get a feeling of freedom and empowerment over their being able to use an "although" or "qualifying" clause in their theses, developing that contrastive paragraph of what others say and then after a transition, going on to state in two or three paragraphs their point of view on the topic. The handout shows a failing essay on human rights in which the student was so caught up

with providing a three part thesis that the last body paragraph, the one that is best remembered in holistic grading, is empty and meaningless. Alternate approaches are provided in Regents' models by Teri Kenith and an anonymous student who both received "3" ratings and reveal the technique of the "although" contrastive or qualifying clause. This "although" clause is praised in the "Instructions for Scoring the Regents' Essays" provided each rater and is referred to as "meritorious" (p. 24) and "clearly more sophisticated" (p. 24).

5. Diagrams of Strategies for Composing the Essay and references to models and detailed analyses (pp. 34–37). Students need to study the in-depth explanations provided on pages 46–58 and practice these options in composing so that they feel the excitement of having increased control over their compositions.

6. Regents' Essay Booklet (simulated) (pp. 39–42).

Students will find two topics printed on the actual Regents' booklet—one within the students' life experience and one outside, requiring knowledge of history, literature, or socio-economic-political issues. Students should choose the one they know most about because no extra credit is given for selecting the more difficult, abstract, or philosophical topic.

Students may choose one of the topics on page 26 to practice writing for sixty minutes if they cannot find time for a practice session in the writing labs or for the mock session announced at the quarterly seminar.

Because the appearance of a full booklet enhances the students' chances of passing the test, students should write in ink on every other line for two pages. If the essayists find they have too much to say, they then can write on every line of the last page. No title is needed. Writers need only to check the box beside the topic chosen.

7. Exercise on Developing a Thesis—with emphasis on the "Although Clause" (p. 43).

During the RTP Seminar students may practice writing the three part formulaic thesis or the "Although Clause" for any of the topics listed. If students plan to use the "Although Clause," they should practice it and develop it in a full length essay. The "Although Clause" should not be complicated and can be very simply constructed as follows:

"Although ($_{some}^{many}$) people are against _____ , I favor it because of _____ and _____ ."

OR

"Although ($_{some}^{many}$) people favor _____ , I am against it because of _____ and _____ ."

The format of the essay would then be the following: the first body paragraph sets forth what others say, and then the student's two major points are developed in five-seven sentences in the second and third paragraphs. A summary conclusion should reflect only the student's point of view.

8. Definition of Expository Essay with Clustering of Major Topics (p. 44).

APPLICATION TO CLASSROOM TEACHING

An effective technique in helping students prepare for the Regents' essay is to have them discuss the major clustering of topics in the form of a panel discussion. Brainstorming the issues and then practicing among themselves are good preparation for presentation of the topics before the class. Then all students can hear about the major clusterings in timed fifteen minute panel discussions evaluated by their fellow students. A timed sixty minute writing session on their topic in a Regents' booklet can be a good introduction to the Regents' essay.

Included on the following pages, pp. 14–15, are "Rules for Panel Discussion" and a "Discussion Evaluation Blank," which are valuable tools to facilitate group discussion in the classroom. The students can choose their top three choices from those topics reflecting the clustering listed on p. 44 of the seminar handout, and the instructor can organize them into discussion groups of no more than five to brainstorm the issue in which they have revealed an interest. Since the students get a choice of three of the ten topics included on the bottom of the definition of the expository essay (p. 44), they are content to focus on one of them in a brainstorming session. During that first meeting they should choose a moderator as indicated by the "Rules." This leader will help to further refine and narrow the issue and will take responsibility for providing an outline for each participant to aid in the class presentation in subsequent class meetings.

After a brief meeting at the beginning of the class day of presentation, the groups' moderators will draw for place on the program. At each presentation, the groups will draw on the blackboard a diagram of their seating arrangement, providing names to correspond with numbers on the "Evaluation Blank." An "Evaluation Blank" should be handed to every member of the audience prior to each presentation, and a timer should be chosen from the class, in full view of the panel, to let the group know how many minutes they have remaining out of the fifteen allotted.

Other instructions include the group members' opening with a suggested introduction or a tentative thesis for the actual writing of the essay which will take place after all discussions have been presented. The group should also be aware that if they do not use their entire fifteen minutes assigned, they may entertain questions from the audience to fill up the remaining time. In assigning a grade for the groups' participation, the instructor simply tallies the scores on the sheets, dividing them by the number of those evaluating and assigning an "A" for (25–21), a "B" for (20–16), a "C" for (15–11), and a similar grade distribution for "D" and "F" grades. The oral presentations usually receive much higher grades than the Regents' essays to follow, so the

12

instructor may want to use the grade as a weekly quiz grade or average it in as 1/4 of the composition grade on the same topic. Before the students write, they are allowed to copy down on the front of the Regents' booklet any notes they may have.

James Britton confirms the importance of this small group, peer interaction in his essay "Talking to Learn" where he observes that "we need to recognize that the network of people related to us by shared values provides, at any stage of life, the primary context for our learning of both varieties—both coming to know and refining our value systems" (106). Certainly, essayists become more aware of the other side of the issue and are more tolerant of others' points of view. Jane Hansen adds in "Organizing Student Learning: Teachers Teach What and How" that "peer writers support each other, protect each other against non-productive forces, and encourage each other's goals" (321). The teacher becomes the coach who helps students get ready for the big game—the Regents' test.

RULES FOR PANEL DISCUSSION

1. There are no formal talks. The method of public conversation is used throughout the meeting of the panel.

2. Individual contributions to the conversation should be brief.

3. Address your remarks to each other, but speak loudly enough so that those in the rear of the room will hear and feel included in the conversation. In this respect, you will have the same problems that confront the actor.

4. You must listen as well as speak. Show by your facial expression and manner that you are paying attention to the other panel members. You can hardly expect audience members to be interested if you and your colleagues seem bored or indifferent.

5. Don't sit back and wait to be called on. If two of you try to speak at once, the leader will decide who is to speak first.

6. If you have three points to make, label them "1", "2", and "3."

7. Sometimes direct your remarks to other panel members: "Bob, what would you say about this situation?" or "I'll have to disagree with you, Joan."

8. Panel members must decide in advance on the following:

   a. Seating arrangement, such as

   b. Length of discussion

   c. Preparing discussion outline

   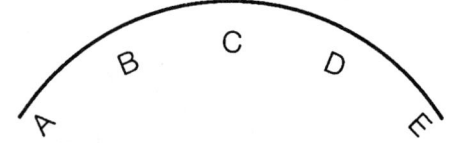

   The planning session should be devoted to an informal discussion of the topic. As the discussion progresses, the leader should note the points made and the evidence offered by each panel member. From these, he/she prepares a tentative outline of the main points which he/she presents to the group for revision and approval before the meeting adjourns. The leader assumes responsibility for expanding the outline and sending a copy to each panel member. The outline should be fastened to a larger sheet of paper on which members make notes of data they wish to present or questions they plan to ask. It is desirable for the panel team to hold a brief session just before presentation to recheck the outline, to make changes or to update the outline, and to review the leader's plan for getting the discussion off to a good start.

DISCUSSION EVALUATION BLANK

Score each speaker from 1 to 5 on each of the five evaluation points described below. The significance of the scores is indicated on the linear scale.

I. Information about the problem (breath, accuracy, use of information).

II. Analysis of the problem (sensing importance, finding theme or issues, avoiding irrelevant matters).

III. Ability to think cooperatively (open mindedness, alertness, willingness to abandon weak arguments, ability to organize and to use arguments of others).

IV. Skill in speaking (adapting voice, action and language to the occasion, ability to state ideas clearly and briefly).

V. Good manners (listening attentively, quoting others accurately, giving others a chance to speak, general courtesy).

(Place name above corresponding letter)

	A	B	C MODERATOR	D	E
1. Information					
2. Analysis					
3. Cooperative thinking					
4. Skills					
5. Good manners					
TOTAL SCORE					
Comments on individual speakers					
Comments on group as a whole					

PART III

THE REGENTS' TEST PREPARATION SEMINAR HANDOUT

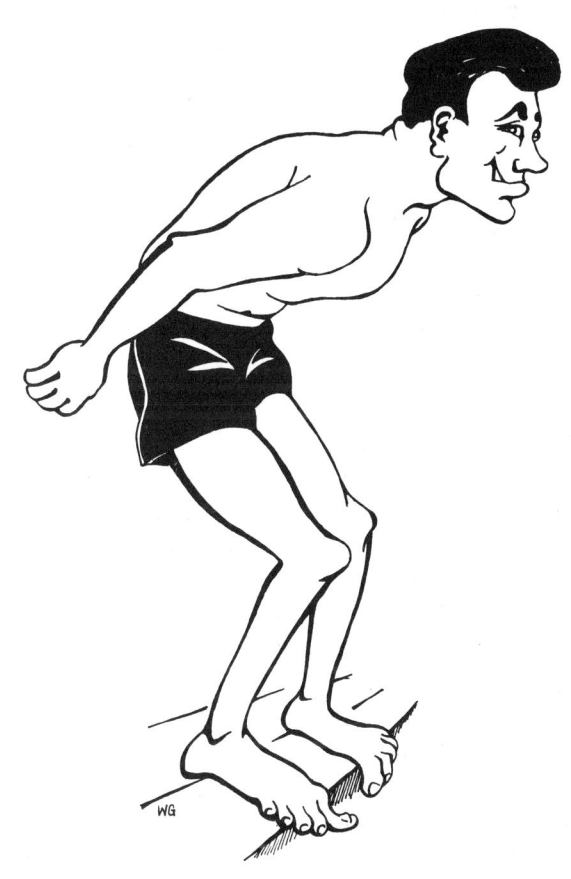

Train for the Big Event

INSTRUCTIONS FOR SCORING REGENTS' TESTING PROGRAM ESSAYS

Description of Essay Scoring Procedure

All graders of the Regents' essays are sent a booklet quarterly to help them prepare to score the Regents' essays and will attend a brief orientation session before the grading session.

Raters should read each essay quickly to gain a general impression of its quality in relation to the model essays and to assign a rating based on that comparison. This approach (the holistic approach) contrasts with the analytical approach which is usual in freshman essay grading, but evidence indicates that holistic grading is much faster and produces more uniform results.

The essays will be rated on a four-point scale in which "1" is the lowest score and "4" is the highest score. The model essays represent borderline cases; each essay to be graded must, by definition, fall above or below a model.

Ratings	4		3		2		1
Models							
		4/3		3/2		2/1	

One model essay represents each dividing line. A essay better then the "2/1" model and worse than the "3/2" would be rated "2." An essay worse than the "2/1" model becomes "1." An essay better then the "4/3" model becomes "4."

Note carefully that raters should compare the essays they read with the models. They should not rate in terms of their usual grading standards or some abstract standard. They should not associate the ratings with the traditional grades A, B, C, D, F.

The testing subcommittee of the University System Academic Committee on English attempts to choose models by using the following definitions of competency, although it realizes that these definitions are by no means exhaustive.

4: The "4" essay has a clear central idea that relates directly to the assigned topic. The essay has a clear organizational plan. The major points are developed logically and are supported with concrete, specific evidence or detail that arouses the reader's interest. The essay reveals the writer's ability to select effective, appropriate words and phrases; to write varied, sophisticated sentences; to make careful use of effective transitional devices; and to maintain a consistent, appropriate tone. The essay is essentially free from mechanical errors, it contains no serious grammatical errors, and the ideas are expressed freshly and vividly.

3: The "3" essay has a clear central idea that relates directly to the assigned topic. It contains most of the qualities of good writing itemized above. The essay generally differs from a "4" in that it shows definite competence, but lacks distinction. The examples and details are pertinent, but may not be particularly vivid or sharply observed; the word choice is generally accurate, but seldom—if ever—really felicitous. The writer adopts an appropriate, consistent tone. The essay may contain a few errors in grammar and mechanics.

2: The "2" essay meets only the basic criteria, and those in a minimal way. The essay has a central idea which is related directly to the assigned topic and which is presented with sufficient clarity that the reader is aware of the writer's purpose. The organization is clear enough for the reader to perceive the writer's plan. The paragraphs coherently present some evidence or details to substantiate the points that are made. The writer uses ordinary, everyday words accurately and idiomatically and generally avoids both the monotony created by series of choppy, simple sentences and the incoherence caused by long, tangled sentences. Although the essay may contain a few serious grammatical errors and several mechanical errors, they are not of sufficient severity or frequency to obscure the sense of what the writer is saying.

1: The "1" essay has any one of the following problems to an extraordinary degree, or it has several to a limited degree: it lacks a central idea; it lacks a clear organizational plan; it does not develop its points or develops them in a repetitious, incoherent, or illogical way; it does not relate directly to the assigned topic; it contains several serious grammatical errors; it contains numerous mechanical errors; ordinary, everyday words are used inaccurately and unidiomatically; it contains a limited vocabulary so that the words chosen frequently do not serve the writer's purpose; syntax is frequently rudimentary or tangled; or the essay is so brief that the rater cannot make an accurate judgment of the writer's ability.

2/1   MODEL   2/1

TOPIC: WHY WOULD YOU LIKE OR DISLIKE OWNING YOUR OWN BUSINESS?

Going out of Business Sale! Signs of this nature can be seen everywhere. Today opening up a business can be scary, because of the extensive risk, high cost, and extreme stress.

The chief reason I would not want to start my own business is the great risk of failure. Today statistics show that four out of every six businesses fail within the first year. Those are not very good odds for one just starting his or her own business.

The second reason not to start my own business is the high cost of starting a business. Businesses take a great deal of money to get started, and for that matter to keep running. The first thing one has to do is find a place to put the business. Lots are very expensive. Then a building had to be built, and merchandise to fill the building has to be purchased.

Finally owning a business can be stressful. Being ones own boss can be stressful to her or him by the way of having to make all of the important decisions, or can cause stress at home. The stress at home can be very detrimental to the marriage, or even the family as a whole.

Concluding this owning a business is just on big headache. On the other hand some people are very successful, and they got that way by taking the risk of owning their own business. I personally don't think that owning a business is worth the risk, when working for someone else is a lot safer.

TOPIC: DISCUSS THE INFLUENCE THAT ADVERTISING HAS HAD ON YOUR LIFE OR THE LIVES OF YOUR FRIENDS.

Advertising has a large influence on my life and the lives of my friends. Advertising has an influence on the cars we drive, the clothes we wear, and the food we eat.

Advertising influences the cars my friends and I drive. The television commercials paint an unrealistic picture of how good life is once you own their product. For example, one of the commercials for Volvo implies that a person doesn't have class unless he drives a Volvo. According to the Cadillac commercial, a car can not be elegant unless it is a Cadillac. Magazine ads are very similar to television ads. Magazine ads show beautiful women and handsome men gathered around an automobile, and imply that the reader can be like the people in the ad.

Advertising has an influence on those clothes we wear. Television and magazines show hair-thin models wearing different articles of clothing. The ads for Jordache or Calvin Klein are a good example of this fact. My friends and I sometimes feel that if the clothes look good, then they must be made good. We also hope the clothes look as good on us as they did on the models.

Finally, advertising influences our eating habits. There are ads for hamburgers, hotdogs, pizzas, beer, candies, cakes, and the list keeps going. Pizza Inn gives us more of the things we like. The people at Burger King treat us right. Everyone wants to be an Oscar Mayer hot dog. Michelob wants us to put a little weekend in our week. Of course, relief is spelled Rolaids. With ads like these facing us every night who could resist?

In conclusion, I'd like to say that advertising influences the way everyone lives. The cars we drive, the clothes we wear, and the food we eat are all a result of advertising.

4/3 MODEL 4/3

TOPIC: DISCUSS WHY PEOPLE ARE FASCINATED BY AMUSEMENT PARKS SUCH AS DISNEY WORLD AND SIX FLAGS.

People of all ages, shapes, sizes, financial statuses, and interests pour, in vast numbers each year into such amusement parks as Disney World and Six Flags. Why the fascination with these places, even to the point of repetitive visits? Each individual has his own reason, but there are a few common to all. Here in a make-believe world can be found something for everyone.

On stepping from a sometimes harsh, ugly world through the gates of a "magic kingdom," one can do for a short while anything he desires. Vicarious living, with all the thrills and dangers of adventure in faraway places or daring escapades unavailable in everyday life, is here for the price of a ticket. There are wild rides: twisting, dipping, now fast, then slow, breath-taking, almost dangerous. For a few minutes one can live on the edge of danger, but always with the knowledge that safety is only inches and seconds away. Tamer rides are available for the children of all ages who prefer their thrills in more sedate doses. There are beautiful, clean, and true-to-life (better than life?) amusements here also; here everything is pretty, always works, and ends before boredom sets in. There are rides that take one through other countries, fantasy worlds, even into a mildly threatening outer space, and always with the surety of a safe return! Threatening animals become friends, and are totally predictable, clean, and nicer than the real thing. One can even return to the past, seeing of course only nostalgic beauty in the "good old days," and handily passing over any unpleasant memories. The future can be attained in seconds, showing the wonders in store for one as a result of the marvelous technilogical advances of mankind.

Of lesser importance, but still a valid reason for amusement park popularity, is the availability of food of many different types. Cuisine of exotic foreign countries is presented in a fairly reasonable form for a decent price. Where else could be tasted a bean-paste sweet typical of Japan, a delicate, flaky Napoleon of France, or a foaming cold beer served in a bier haus of Germany? All this, and more, is available at one price, as often as wished.

So are seen two reasons for the tremendous popularity of the amusement parks. All in one package, for one price, instant gratification is there, every day, year-round. All need and desire escape from mundane lives. The amusement parks provide this escape.

ANALYSIS OF MODEL ESSAYS

Analysis of 2/1 Model

The essay is not a clear "2" because only the third paragraph is adequately developed; the next-to-the-last sentence of the essay violates the unity and coherence of the paragraph in which it appears; several phrases are unidiomatic; some words and phrases are repeated excessively; the second sentence of the fourth paragraph contains a jarring shift in construction; throughout the essay the point of view vacillates between the first person and the third; and in the first sentence of the last paragraph, "concluding this," a dangling modifier, is particularly confusing because "this" lacks a referent and the phrase is not set off with a comma.

The essay is not a clear "1" because it has a central idea that directly answers the question raised by the topic and that is developed through a clear organizational plan; the transitions are clear, although blatant and conventional; the third paragraph is reasonably coherent, logical, and free from repetition; the essay contains only a few serious grammatical errors, no spelling errors, and no errors in diction that block communication; the syntax is neither consistently rudimentary nor hopelessly tangled; and the essay has an interest-catching opening.

Analysis of 3/2 Model

The essay demonstrates more than the "minimal competence" of a "2" essay but fails to attain the "definite competence" of a "3." Although the central idea is related to the topic, this idea is not always in clear focus: details, particularly in the second paragraph, describe more the appeals than the effects of advertisements. The opening paragraph has no introduction, merely the thesis divided into two sentences, and the conclusion is a gratuitous restatement of the opening. Transitional phrases are either non-existent or uninspired.

The essay rates above a "2" because it has clear organization, adequate development, and parallel structure. Details are vivid, occasionally novel, and the point of view and tone are generally consistent, the latter being lightly ironic. With the exception of the overuse and misuse of "good" in paragraph three, the extraneous comma in paragraph two, and the necessary comma omitted from paragraph four, word choice is accurate and punctuation correct. Grammatically the essay is altogether sound.

Analysis of 4/3 Model

The essay is not quite a "4" chiefly because the organizational plan is rather ineffective. The second paragraph lacks a clear focus—given the variety of details contained in it, the writer might very well have gone on to discuss food along with the rides, the animals, and the nostalgic vistas. Of less importance, in the second sentence of the second paragraph, the verb should be nearer its subject; transitional devices are not used skillfully; the writer overuses the "there are" construction in the second paragraph; "technological" is misspelled; and punctuation is sometimes questionable.

The essay is better than a "3" because some of the details are sharply—or wryly—observed; the writer turns some nice phrases; the writer manifests a certain sophistication in diction as reflected in the correct use of "sedate," "vicarious," and "gratification"; and the essay contains no grammatical or mechanical errors and only one spelling error.

QUESTIONS AND ANSWERS ON THE RATING OF REGENTS' TEST ESSAYS

1. Why do we have 2/1, 3/2, and 4/3 models? Why don't we have models of "1," "3," and "4" essays?

All of the discrete ratings cover a wide range of writing performance, particularly the "1." An essay may be assigned a "1" because it is only one sentence long, because it is off the topic, because it contains grammatical errors that frustrate the writer's attempt to communicate, because it is totally lacking in structure, because its points are undeveloped, and so on. There are very, very low "1's," and there are "1's" that are almost passing. While "2," "3," and "4" do not cover so wide a range, it would still be impossible simply to pick one model and say, "This is it." The example would, of necessity, be a low "3," a middling "3," or a high "3." The 4/3, 3/2, and 2/1 models are intended to represent a very fine borderline.

2. What specifically does the 2/1 model represent?

The essay chosen as a 2/1 model represents the absolute balance point between the "1" and the "2" essay. The committee which selected the essay would hope that, if the 2/1 model essay were rated by fifty raters, it would receive twenty-five "1's" and twenty-five "2's." A tiny nudge could swing the balance either way. It would be a clear "2," if, for example: a few more supporting details were supplied, the diction were more appropriate, the mechanical and grammatical errors were fewer, or the coherence were improved. On the other hand, it would be a clear "1" if it were a trifle weaker in any one of these aspects.

3. Must an essay have a thesis sentence to pass?

Not necessarily. Although an explicit thesis sentence is perfectly acceptable, and many—perhaps most—of our students need one, many a good writer can make the implied thesis clear and can organize the essay well enough so that the reader can follow the line of thought without the writer's having revealed the organizational plan in the introductory paragraph.

4. Must the essay follow a set formula?
No.

5. What should be done with essays that are off the topic?

We face two problems here. One involves the student who has a prepared essay and tries to fit it to the topic; the other involves the student who misreads or misunderstands the topic. When raters find an essay that is completely off the topic, they must fail the essay. Misreading is more problematic. Many students who wrote on the topic "Children should never be disciplined by corporal punishment. Defend or attack the statement." thought that corporal punishment was the same as capital punishment. Similarly, a few students who wrote on the topic "Name two or three qualities which you feel a person should possess in order to be a good employee." discussed qualities of a good employer rather than a good employee. When a writer misreads the topic this grossly, the essay should be failed. Most of the misreadings, however, are not so blatant. Many raters found themselves perplexed by the responses to the following two topics: "Discuss the most important moral qualities an elected official should have." and "What qualities of character do you regard as important in a person you would choose as a friend?" Students writing on the latter topic would blithely talk about how their friends should have good looks, an effervescent personality, and plenty of money more often (or so it seemed) than they would talk about qualities of character such as honesty, integrity, and trustworthiness. Much of the same was true of the former topic, where students would talk about charisma, intelligence, and charm. Seldom, if ever, was an essay totally off the topic: a typical thesis sentence might read "My friends should be loyal, intelligent, honest, and easy to get along with." The raters must penalize the essay for this type of misunderstanding, but such an essay should not be failed out of hand. If the essay is well-written and the student does not seem to be deliberately evading the topic, the essay might well deserve one of the passing scores.

The question of whether the writer can both attack and defend an issue when the topic says "attack or defend" has been raised. When the student deals with pro and con arguments but takes a clear stand on one side of the issue, the answer is definitely yes. Doing so is not merely acceptable, it is meritorious: "although the 55 mph speed limit costs motorists some time and encourages many citizens to break the law, it should be retained because it saves lives, conserves gas, and reduces the number and severity of accidents" is clearly more sophisticated than "the 55 mph speed limit should be retained because it saves money, lives, and gasoline." The student who simply attacks and defends without coming down on one side or the other does imperil the chances of passing. However, the student who writes a good fence-straddling essay should be passed.

6. May the student modify the topic?

Students may make reasonable modifications of the topic. For example, given the topic "What courses that you did not take in high school do you now wish you had taken?" students may state that there are no such courses and explain why. Also, students do not have to discuss specific courses, but may state that they should have taken more courses in an area such as English or history.

Students should not be penalized for narrowing the topic. For example, given a topic which asks for a discussion of the goals of the women's liberation movement, students could narrow the topic by discussing only economic issues.

Students may handle the topic in the first person or the third person, regardless of the person in which the topic is stated. For example, given the topic "Do you agree with the goals of the women's liberation movement?" students may answer, "The goals of the women's liberation movement are valid," and continue in the third person.

7. How should the rater react to obviously spurious statistics and obviously counterfeit examples?

We must keep in mind that the student writing for the Regents' Test does not have access to an almanac or a set of encyclopedias. Raters should, therefore, be very patient with approximate statistics and with dubious uncles. At the same time, raters must keep in mind that, to the extent examples and statistics are incredible, they are rhetorically ineffective and thus lessen the essay's chances of passing. Writers who say that the accident rate dropped by approximately 10% after the 55 mph speed limit was put into effect strengthen their case; writers who say that the accident rate was cut in half when the 55 mph speed limit was put into effect weaken theirs.

24

8. How should we rate an essay of comic or satiric intent?
Reward the successful and penalize the inept.

GUIDELINES FOR WRITING THE REGENTS' ESSAY

The instructions stress four tasks:

1. State and develop a central idea

2. Organize to show an overall plan

3. Deal with the assigned topic

4. Avoid errors

Use the space provided on the front of the essay booklet for making brief notes. Write down your ideas for developing the central idea so that you can choose the best ideas, see where you need additional ideas, and decide how to order/organize the ideas.

Write the essay:

1. on every other line of the booklet

2. in pen (REQUIRED)

3. in the suggested time frame:
   5–10 minutes to choose the topic and plan the essay;
   5 minutes to write the introduction;
   30 minutes to write the support paragraphs and the conclusion;
   15 minutes to proofread and edit.

REGENTS' ESSAY TOPICS

(Samples from the list of 493 approved topics)
Choose one and apply guidelines.

1. Should both parents assume equal responsibility for child rearing?

2. "The United States should greatly increase its support of mass transit systems." Attack or defend.

3. "College students benefit from having to earn at least part of their tuition." Agree or disagree.

4. How has the study of the natural sciences affected your understanding of the world and the way you approach day-to-day living? Explain.

ANALYSIS OF REGENTS' ESSAY/CONTENT/FORM/MECHANICS

NAME _____

DATE _____

	DATE AND TOPIC OF ESSAY	
CONTENT		
***Essay addresses the topic.		
Ideas are logical.		
Ideas are clearly expressed.		
ORGANIZATION		
***Thesis is present in the essay.		
* Thesis is stated in introduction.		
* Stated order is followed.		
Thesis is adequately developed.		
** Each support paragraph is developed with appropriate, concrete details.		
Each support paragraph has a controlling idea.		
** The essay follows the five paragraph model.		
MECHANICS		
Handwriting is legible.		
Punctuation errors are not serious.		
* Verbs are used correctly.		
* Pronouns are used correctly.		
***Subjects and verbs agree.		
* Nouns and pronouns agree.		
** Spelling is correct.		
Words are used correctly.		
Sentences are not awkward.		
***Essay is free of fragments.		
***Essay is free of run-on and comma splices.		

(Items are marked with * to indicate importance.)

AN EXAMPLE OF WHAT YOU <u>DO NOT</u> WANT TO WRITE FOR THE REGENTS' ESSAY

There are three things that I like about the South. First, there are friendly people living in the South. Second, the weather in the South is pleasant. Finally, there are many historical sites in the South which are interesting.

There are friendly people living in the South. Most people in the South are very pleasant. They are also helpful and understanding. People in the South tend to go out of their way in order to help a friend in need. Southern people seem to have a natural talent for their friendliness and hospitality.

The weather in the South is pleasant. The South hardly ever experiences bad storms. The weather in the South is very predictable. The weather in the South hardly ever brings about a drastic change in the environment. The pleasant weather in the South allows one to live in a comfortable atmosphere.

There are many historical sites in the South which are interesting. Stone Mountain of Georgia is an interesting historical site in the South. The Little White House is another one of Georgia's interesting historical sites of the South. The historical sites of the South are interesting because they tell a lot about the South's past. The historical sites of the South serve as a learning experience for its viewers.

In conclusion, there are three things that I like about the South. First, there are friendly people living in the South. Second, the weather in the South is pleasant. Finally, there are many historical sites in the South which are interesting.

A Clown Act Or A Five Paragraph Essay, It's Up To You

Thesis (This is the main point of your paper that you'd better not let break!)

Introductory Paragraph

The Body (This is the bulk of your paper. It has to support & balance your thesis.)

Concluding Paragraph (This repeats what you have said throughout your paper. It has to be strong and must sum up the point of your thesis.)

REGENTS' ESSAY CHECKLIST

Practice Regents'
Essays
(Use a '✓' or 'O' in
response to questions

			1st	2nd	3rd
(1st paragraph)		Are there three sentences before the thesis?			
		Are they varied in structure and length?			
		Do they lead naturally into the thesis?			
I. INTRODUCTION		Is a thesis present?			
(40–50 words)		Is it divided into three parts?			
		Are those parts parallel?			
		Are there SHARP divisions?			
		Are those divisions punctuated correctly?			
(2nd, 3rd, 4th paragraphs)		Is a topic sentence present in each body paragraph?			
		Does the topic sentence relate to the thesis?			
II. BODY		Are there 5–7 sentences per paragraph?			
(100–150 words per developmental paragraph)		Are there 100–150 words per paragraph?			
		Do the paragraphs contain detailed, specific material?			
* DIVISION OF TIME		Does the body contain relevant material?			
10 minutes to plan (including 5 min. for thesis) 10 minutes per paragraph 5 minutes for conclusion, 10 minutes for proofreading		Does it avoid repetition of idea?			
		Does the body of the essay hold the reader's attention?			
		Are there transitions between paragraphs?			
III. CONCLUSION		Is a conclusion present?			
		Does it reaffirm the thesis?			
		Does it give the paper a note of finality?			
IV. MECHANICS		Is essay free of fragments?			
		Is essay free of run-on and comma splices?			
		Do all subjects and verbs agree?			
		Is all spelling correct?			
		Are verbs used correctly?			
		Are pronouns used correctly?			
		Do nouns and pronouns agree?			
		Are words used correctly?			
		Are sentences clearly written?			
		Is handwriting legible?			
		Is essay free of serious punctuation errors?			
V. Did writer follow suggested division of time? (See * above)					

(Students may want to exchange essays for peer evaluation.) CORRECTED BY _____.

ANALYSIS OF FORMULAIC FAILING ESSAY

"Human rights" is a term frequently used but seldom defined. What rights should belong to every human being? Discuss.

There are many human rights that all people should be able to have. In our country, we have certain inalienable rights that belong to everyone. I believe that all human beings should have freedom of choice, freedom of speech, and freedom of liberty.

To begin with, all human beings should have freedom of choice. I believe that it is up to the individual to make his own decisions. For example, abortion is a very controversial topic. I believe that choice of abortion should be left up to the parents of the unborn child. Many people believe that abortion should not be legalized. If abortion is not legalized, then the parents of the unborn child are not given a choice. I believe this is unfair and unconstitutional. Every person should be able to make his own decisions, right or wrong.

Next, every human being should have freedom of speech. All humans should be able to voice their own opinion. If people were not allowed to speak freely, where would our world be today? For example, if freedom of speech were not allowed in the United States, slavery would have never been abolished. People stood up for what they believed, and because of that, blacks are free people today. Through his speeches, Martin Luther King, Jr. got the black race the rights that they deserve.

Finally, all people should have freedom of liberty. Every person in the world should be able to have liberty and to be free. All people should be able to make their own decisions. A person should be able to live his life freely. For example, every American has the right to live the life that he wants to live. All Americans are allowed to vote for their government officials. In some places of the world, freedom of liberty is not given to individuals. I believe that the right of liberty should be given to everyone.

In conclusion, all human beings deserve to have certain rights. Three rights that all human beings should have are freedom of choice, freedom of speech, and freedom of liberty.

(Failing Essay) (1) rating

Students trapped in the formulaic approach of three sharp divisions of the thesis may find themselves writing empty paragraphs. Alternatives include an extended example or narrative to illustrate a particular point or the contrastive paragraph which is predicted by the "although" or "qualifying" clause in the thesis. This last approach is praised on page 24 of the instructors' directions for scoring the Regents' essays.

Essays Illustrating "Although Clause"

Teri Kenith failed the Regents' essay because she had difficulty in finding enough to say about her topic. Then she practiced and mastered the "although" clause in her thesis which predicts contrasting arguments for one body paragraph. She felt a sense of relief from the tyranny of the formulaic thesis, knowing that for one paragraph she could discuss what other people say and then go on to develop her <u>two</u> main points.

Support for Our Olympic Teams

TERI KENITH

English 101, Practice Regents' Essay
Topic: "Should the government subsidize our Olympic teams?"
Why or why not?

Narrative intro.

WALKING THE STREETS AT THIS VERY MOMENT IS AN OLYMPIC STAR—not a current star, mind you, but a young man or woman who has the potential to become one of our brightest Olympic talents. Chances are, though, that this person will never do much more in life than grill hamburgers or press shirts at a dry cleaners, and the reason for this is pure and simple: money. <u>Although there are many valid arguments against the government's financial support of our Olympic teams, subsidizing would help to insure a stronger and more talented team and would also help to promote pride in our nation.</u>

"Although," contrasting clause in thesis.

Certainly, there are many valid arguments against the government's subsidizing the Olympics. Opponents argue that there are millions of people in the United States living below the poverty line. They argue that we need to build a strong defense and that there are already too many free hand-outs. The four trillion dollar federal deficit is another point of the opposition. With that debt hanging over our heads, who needs to spend more? Of course, the rising and seemingly uncontrollable crime rate is another protest. Many feel that improved law enforcement and modern prisons should be the nation's number one priority. <u>These are all valid negative aspects of spending more on the Olympics, but the positive arguments far outweigh the negative.</u>

Contrasting paragraph

Important transition leading to Teri's two arguments

If we did subsidize the Olympic teams, we would have stronger and more talented teams. Those talented young people who aren't able to train properly because of lack of funding would be able to train and perfect their talents. Russia's athletes receive paid training during their whole athletic career and it shows. They always seem to earn more medals than any other country. Also, if the government subsidized the teams, we might have larger and more versatile teams. In case one star athlete were injured, another could take his/her place.

Teri's argument

31

Teri's argument

Our pride in our nation's performance is also sorely lacking. As well as our teams do now, think of the added pride our nation would be feeling if we did even better. With more and better trained athletes, we are bound to fare even better in the competition. This increased pride that America would be feeling would allow us to project confidence to the rest of the world. The world might then accord us the respect that we have somehow lost. Winning in international competition gives us and other nations the feeling that our form of government promotes excellence. Moreover, competing successfully on the playing field might obviate the need for building bigger and better missiles to prove our national prowess.

Conclusion

Happy ending—Teri received a 3 on the actual Regents' test.

The Olympic teams are our source of pride and accomplishment, and we should encourage their success by whatever means is available. They are our showcase to the rest of the world. They are a peaceful way to project what America is all about—freedom and excellence.

This example of an alternate approach to the formulaic three part thesis was used by the Regents' professor conducting the graders' workshop prior to the rating session held quarterly. This actual Regents' essay received a <u>3</u> or "above average" rating by the graders.

Should Georgia legalize gambling to raise more revenue? Discuss.

Qualifying or contrasting clause

For many years, gambling has been a controversial issue within many state governments. The question of the legalization of gambling is not an easy one. Some states, such as Nevada, have chosen to legalize gambling as a means of additional revenue. Other states, such as Georgia, have not legalized gambling for many reasons including moral issues and concern about public welfare. <u>Even though there may be some economical advantages to legalizing gambling in Georgia</u>, the overall effects of gambling in the lives of however many compulsive gamblers there may be in Georgia would ruin these people, their families, and their friends and invite organized crime.

Development of contrasting clause (What other people say)

Transition

Gambling can be a good source of revenue in some states by providing extra money that the government might not have had otherwise. This money may be spent on the educational system, public utilities or any type of community programs. In addition to its economical advantages, gambling is also enjoyable entertainment for many people. What people fail to see is the destruction in the lives of the people for whom this entertainment becomes a habit they cannot break.

Development of first point by author

The life of a compulsive gambler can be destroyed in so many ways. A man may lose his job because he is falling behind in office work worrying about where all his money has gone. If the gambler loses all of his savings and no longer has a job, he cannot provide for his family or himself and may fall deeper into debt with no way out. If a gambler borrows money to gamble or even to pay back gambling debts, he may still find himself unable to keep any money to live on. This problem will not only affect him, but also his children and wife will be harmed by his problem. If gambling were legalized, this vicious cycle of behavior would be an easier trap to fall into than it already is. Look at the statistics of compulsive gambling in Georgia when gambling is not even legal yet. How many more people would fall prey to gambling? How many more lives would be ruined?

Development of second point by author

Besides the effects on the personal lives of gambling victims, another negative aspect of gambling is crime. In cities such as Las Vegas and Atlantic City, the organized crime rate is astounding. Do Georgians want the mob or loan sharks roaming their cities? There is enough crime to deal with already without worrying about more coming in as a result of legalizing gambling.

Conclusion

Georgia has had a good record of economy for many years. Why should Georgia allow people to possibly risk their lives, homes, families, jobs, and safety over an entertaining pastime? The revenue is not worth it. If gambling is so important to some people, then they can always get on a plane to Atlantic City, because Georgia does not need gambling to keep its economy alive.

DIAGRAMS OF STRATEGIES FOR COMPOSING THE REGENTS' ESSAY AND REFERENCES TO MODELS AND DETAILED ANALYSES

I. THE FORMULAIC APPROACH

See pages 46–47 for model and analyses

Contextual introduction

1. _____
2. _____
3. _____

Three sentences leading to the thesis

Broad ideas narrowed to a thesis

Thesis _____ X   X   X (three parts)
Save best point to last

Three body paragraphs

Transitions between paragraphs

1st body paragraph

Topic sentence
5-7 sentences
150 words

2nd body paragraph

Topic sentence
5-7 sentences
150 words

3rd body paragraph

Topic sentence
5-7 sentences
150 words

(Best point developed)

Summary / conclusion

3 or 4 sentences

Structure • Two Part Thesis • Although Clause Strategy • Formulaic • Descriptive • Narrative

WG

34

II. THE STRUCTURED OPENING OPTION

See pages 47–50 for model and analyses

Sharp divisions

1st idea ————————

2nd idea ————————

3rd idea ————————

Structured introduction

Unifying thesis

3 body paragraphs

Transitions

1st body paragraph — 1st idea developed 5-7 sentences, 150 words

2nd body paragraph — 2nd idea developed 5-7 sentences, 150 words

Most powerful paragraph

3rd body paragraph — 3rd idea developed 5-7 sentences, 150 words

Summary / conclusion

3 or 4 sentences

III. THE TWO PART THESIS WITH A SUBDIVISION OR EXTENDED EXAMPLE

See pages 50–52 for model and analyses

Contrastive Introduction

Two part thesis   X   X

1st idea developed
5-7 sentences, 150 words

2nd idea developed, subdivided into two parts

Use of unifying references

Use of Transitions

1st point

5-7 sentences
150 words

2nd point

5-7 sentences
150 words

Strongest point

Conclusion - restatement of thesis

IV. THE CONTRASTIVE PARAGRAPH OR "ALTHOUGH CLAUSE" STRATEGY

See pages 53–55 for model and analyses

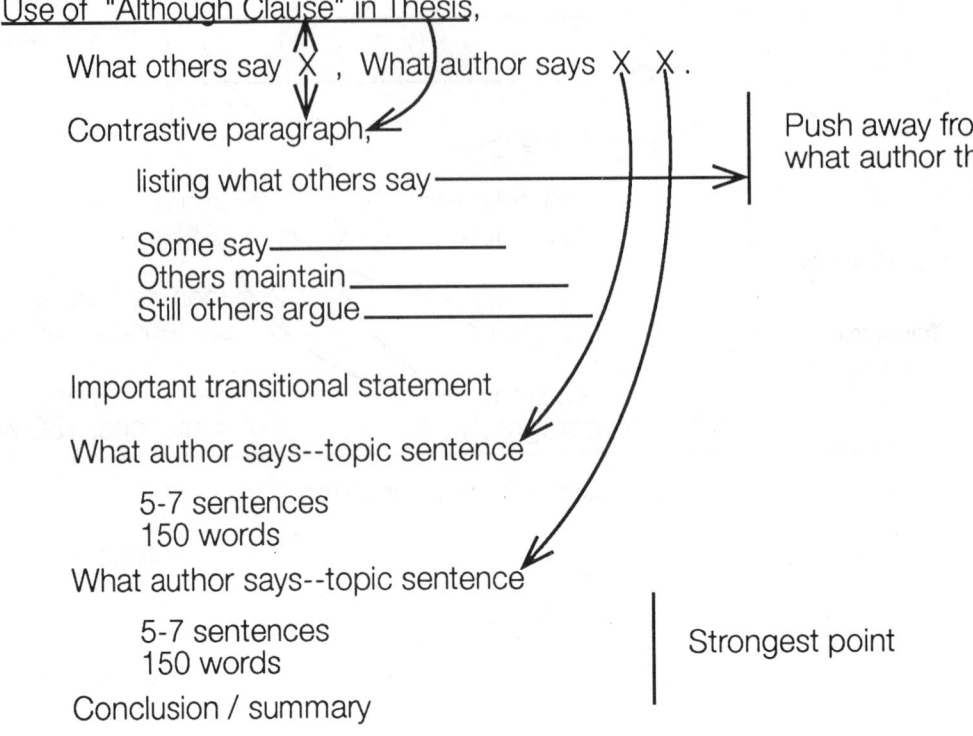

Narrative opening

Use of "Although Clause" in Thesis,

What others say X , What author says X X .

Contrastive paragraph;

listing what others say

Some say————————
Others maintain——————
Still others argue——————

Push away from what author thinks.

1st body paragraph

Important transitional statement

What author says--topic sentence

5-7 sentences
150 words

2nd body paragraph

Transitions between paragraphs

What author says--topic sentence

5-7 sentences
150 words

3rd body paragraph

Strongest point

Conclusion / summary

3-4 sentences

V. NARRATIVE AND DESCRIPTIVE OPTIONS

(Organize by time and order.)   (Appeal to the senses.)

See pages 55–58 for models and analyses.

VI. OPTIONS FOR INTRODUCTIONS
(at least three sentences before thesis)
  a. Time Line—(past to present) leading to a thesis
  b. Narrative—(story intro) leading to a thesis
  c. Contextual—broad ideas narrowed to a thesis
  d. Contrastive—("some say"—"others maintain") leading to a thesis
  e. Descriptive—(using appeal to the senses, describing person or place) leading to a thesis
  f. Structured—(using three ideas plus a unifying thesis with those ideas developed into subsequent paragraphs)

USA TODAY AS A TEACHING TOOL

The USA Today is a useful resource for teaching the Regents' Preparation course or for preparing to write the Regents' essay because it presents a debate page daily and allows a student to see that experts have logical, documented arguments on both sides of an issue. These issues, almost without exception, are included in the 493 topics listed as the "Approved Regents' Test Essay Topics," starting on page 123. Students can read the articles and create a thesis—either the three part formulaic approach or the "Although Clause" strategy. After discussing the issues in small groups in a composition class, the students are mentally prepared through inquiry to write an informed, developed essay.

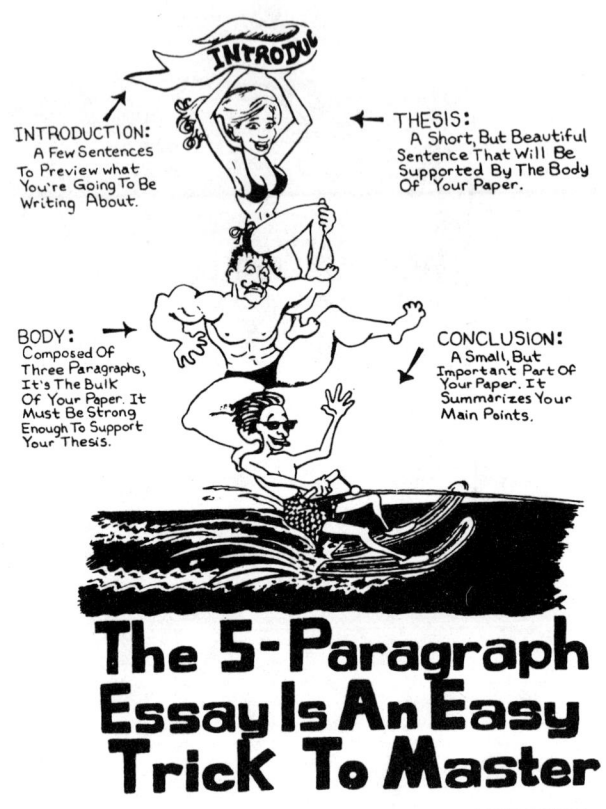

INTRODUCTION:
A Few Sentences
To Preview what
You're Going To Be
Writing About.

THESIS:
A Short, But Beautiful
Sentence That Will Be
Supported By The Body
Of Your Paper.

BODY:
Composed Of
Three Paragraphs,
It's The Bulk
Of Your Paper. It
Must Be Strong
Enough To Support
Your Thesis.

CONCLUSION:
A Small, But
Important Part Of
Your Paper. It
Summarizes Your
Main Points.

The 5-Paragraph Essay Is An Easy Trick To Master

WALT GRIFFIN

REGENTS' TESTING PROGRAM ESSAY BOOKLET (60 Minutes)

SOCIAL SECURITY NUMBER

☐☐☐ – ☐☐ – ☐☐☐☐

Using your pen, write your social security number in the boxes at the top of the page. Choose one of the following; put an "X" in the box to indicate your choice.

Begin your essay on the first lined page. You may use the space below for an outline or notes. Don't write your essay here. Use this space to prepare. Planning an essay for at least ten minutes will aid you in passing the test. Brainstorm! Jot down ideas related to the topic; visualize yourself in the topic; construct a main idea, and cluster details. Leave time to proof for major errors. Remember you can use a dictionary (your own) during the last fifteen minutes announced.

Page 1)

WORKSHEET ON REGENTS' EXAMINATION TOPICS

Name _____

Select one and develop a thesis:

*1. Although clause suggested—jot down pros and cons to find your side. Should the United States pass gun control laws? Why or why not?
Thesis: _____

_____

2. Describe the influence that advertising has had on your life and the life of your friends. Explain and evaluate this statement.
Thesis: _____

_____

*3. Although clause suggested—jot down pros and cons to find your side. Georgia should legalize gambling to raise more revenue. Why or why not?
Thesis: _____

_____

4. Explain why you would or would not want to live in a large city.
Thesis: _____

_____

5. What changes would occur in your lifestyle if you were forced to live in a cash economy?
Thesis: _____

_____

6. Is it beneficial for a high school graduate to work full-time for a year before entering college? Why or why not?
Thesis: _____

THE EXPOSITORY ESSAY

An expository theme is the most common theme style used in developing the Regents' topics. Exposition can contain definitions, comparison and contrast, examples, facts, incidents, and arguments. It often combines several techniques used in types of themes that you have already written in composition classes. In all expository essays, you will carefully construct a thesis sentence in the first paragraph or introduction and will support it with paragraphs. The thesis will predict and control your essay development.

An expository essay can be compared with a discussion. Just as the class will have panel discussions and will explore all aspects of a topic, so you shall be composing a thesis statement and developing it thoroughly. An argumentative theme can be compared with a debate. Just as debaters must take a stand and must attempt to convince the audience to their way of thinking, so writers of an argumentative essay must adopt a definite side and write to persuade their readers. Therefore, the difference between an expository and an argumentative essay is that an expository theme does not necessarily contain a definite stand; the writer analyzes the entire issue. Sometimes the writers present their ideas and let the reader decide, but in writing a passing Regents' essay, the writers are expected to come to a careful conclusion after considering various aspects of the topic. Thus, writers of expository themes do not write with the purpose of convincing the readers but with the idea of informing them.

Transitions used in an expository essay are as follows: and, or/nor, also, moreover, furthermore, indeed, in fact, first, second, for instance, for example, for one thing, similarly, likewise, therefore, thus, so, and so, hence, consequently, finally, on the whole, all in all, in other words, in short, frequently, occasionally, in particular, in general, specifically, especially, usually, of course, no doubt, doubtless, to be sure, granted (that), certainly, but, however, yet, on the contrary, not at all, surely, no, still, nevertheless, not withstanding, although, though, whereas, because, since, for, if, provided, in case, unless, lest, when, as if, as though, even if.

These discussion topics reflect the major clustering of the 493 published Regents' topics:

1. What's Happening to the American Family? (55–60)

2. The Quality of Television (50–55)

3. Public School Education in the United States—Strengths and Weaknesses (65–70)

4. The Economic State of the Nation (25–30)

5. Growing Old in America (45–50)

6. Crime—Cause or Prevention (55–60)

7. America's Role in the Free World (25–30)

8. The Defense of the United States (15–20)

9. Health and Physical Fitness (40–45)

10. The State of the Environment (10–15)

PART IV

ANALYSES OF REGENTS' ESSAYS

THE FORMULAIC APPROACH

The first Regents' essay used in the seminar is Alice A. Zeigler's "Why Don't We Respect Congress?" This essay exemplifies what is termed as the formulaic response to a Regents' topic. It follows very closely the model of the five paragraph theme:

- The contextual introduction includes three sentences before the thesis—from the general to the specific.

- The thesis is one sentence with a sharp division of three aspects of the topic.

- Each part of the thesis introduces a new paragraph.

- Each paragraph has a topic sentence.

- Specific detail in five-seven sentences or 150 words develops the topic.

- Transitional expressions are used within and between paragraphs to unify the essay.

- A summary ending of approximately four sentences is provided.

Formula example Contextual introduction Broad ideas narrowed to thesis General statements narrowed to the specific 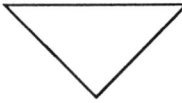 Three sentences before the thesis THESIS—three parts, sharp divisions First part of thesis Topic sentence 5–7 sentences or 150 words Transitions and pronouns provide unity.	**"Why Don't We Respect Congress?"** <u>ALICE A. ZEIGLER</u> English 101, Practice Regents' Essay Topic: Discuss two or three possible causes for the decline in respect for the United States Congress in recent years. THE CONGRESS OF THE UNITED STATES IS A VERY POWERFUL group of men and women. Many of our representatives to Congress have been there for long periods of time; however, in most recent elections, many of the long-term people have been turned out and replaced by new faces. One of the reasons for this turnover is the decline of respect felt by voters for their representatives. <u>Voters in this country and governments around the world have lost respect for the United States Congress as a result of their illegal activities, their mudslinging tactics, and their inability to take action.</u> Over the past several years, authorities within the government have exposed illegal activities among members of Congress. <u>Some of these activities</u> include prostitution, illegal financial deals, and bribes accepted from lobbyists or special interest groups. <u>One of the</u> first major scandals involved a Congressman who was providing sumptuous living arrangements, fine clothes, and other benefits for a well-known prostitute. <u>Another</u> Congressman was filmed accepting a large sum of money and promising his vote in return. <u>The most</u>

recent scandals have involved either participation in or failure to report financial activities which are prohibited due to conflicts of interest. When Americans elect a man or woman to a position of power and influence, they expect that person to duplicate their own high ideals. When these ideals are not as high as their own, they tend to lose respect. [Through her sharp divisions of the topic, Alice Zeigler avoids repetition of detail, a major reason for a poor rating.]

[Transition]

Another reason for declining respect is the mudslinging tactics used during campaigns, when battling a particularly touchy subject or when trying to discredit an opponent. Leaders in government seem unable to find valid, sound reasons for opposing someone. They fail to define their thinking on the issues so they resort to character assassination as a means of getting elected. In some cases it takes very careful digging (sometimes illegally) to find just the right discrediting information. Office holders have even been accused of hiring private detectives to spy on their competitors. Finding discrediting information not only detracts from the competitor but also makes the mudslinger himself look petty and small.

Finally, each session of Congress seems to end with a large number of bills which have not been acted upon. This inactivity happens often when an issue is especially touchy, and Congress is afraid or unwilling to take a stance. Their lack of accomplishment also carries over to their dealings with a President. For instance, when a President presents a budget, Congress resorts to name-calling, infighting, and other tactics which delay passing a budget instead of working together in a unified manner to achieve goals which would benefit the nation as a whole. Re-election and the need for power seem to be more important than the passing of vital legislation which would move the nation forward.

The decline of respect for men and women in Congress grows each time a new scandal breaks. Power, rather than honesty and decency, seems to drive the representatives. Illegal activities, mudslinging tactics, and lack of accomplishment have set the standards in recent years, making respect a lost commodity.

Since the essay is rated independently and holistically by three raters, it is important to place the most powerful point in the last body paragraph.

THE STRUCTURED OPENING OPTIONS

Another essay utilized in the Regents' seminar, "The Denial of Human Rights" by Mike Steger, illustrates what is referred to as the structured opening. Three aspects of the topic are introduced sentence by sentence and are later developed into body paragraphs; however, a unifying thesis must still be present. Specific examples of not only the international violation of human rights but also a local problem give the essay depth and maturity. Transitions are present within paragraphs and between them to give unity and coherence to the writing. Again the student placed what he considered to be the most important point last, and a conclusion of approximately four sentences gives the essay a sense of closure.

"The Denial of Human Rights"

MIKE STEGER
English 101, Practice Regents' Essay
Topic: Human Rights is a term frequently used but seldom defined.
What rights should belong to every human being?

A RUSSIAN CITIZEN, STUDYING HIS BELIEF IN JUDAISM, IS persecuted for this belief. A black citizen in South Africa is denied his right to hold a job equal to that of a white citizen in South Africa. A black family buys a house in an all-white neighborhood, and they have to move after one night because their children are harassed and their house is fire-bombed. These are harsh, but basic examples that illustrate the denial of basic human rights to worship freely and to live and work without discrimination—rights which all persons should be allowed to possess.

For many years, Russian Jews have been denied numerous rights and privileges simply because of their religious beliefs. The right to practice the faith of their choice is a right which all men should have. When a person is segregated from society simply because of what he believes, there is cause for alarm. The Russian Communist Party has a rude awakening coming if it believes persons who practice the Jewish faith can be a threat to the Party. The mind is one thing that cannot be controlled. This minority group fighting the persecution should be allowed to worship as should all human beings, without their lives and day-to-day existence being threatened.

Yet, this is not the only region on this planet where persons are denied their basic rights. The black citizens of South Africa are in a constant struggle to obtain their human rights. Unlike the Russians, who are persecuted for their religious beliefs, the South Africans are persecuted because their skin is of a different color. For generations, blacks in South Africa have been ruled by the white society. This rule, which parallels dictatorship, has been the accepted form of government since the first explorers discovered this rich and abundant resource region of Africa. The white man, refined and educated in Europe, considered the blacks to be illiterate, barbaric and less than human. This harsh segregation continues even today. The South African Anglican Bishop, Bishop Tutu, is desperately fighting the racial bias in his country. He states that the blacks in South Africa are becoming aliens in the land of their birth and that if this policy of unequality doesn't halt soon, it will end up like Hitler's solution for the Jews. This is the twentieth century, where all men are supposed to be equal. Yet simply because these persons are black, they are denied the rights which should be theirs.

However, this denial is not exclusive to South Africa. Black persons in our communities are being denied their rights every day.

3rd idea

Unifying references

Most powerful paragraph

<u>They</u> are even being denied the basic right to live where they please. <u>For example</u>, last spring, a black family moved into a predominantly white neighborhood in Cobb County. <u>This area</u> has been an all-white community since its development and a community with few or no incidents of crime or violence. However, the first night <u>this family</u> stayed in their new home, it was fire-bombed. <u>Additionally</u>, earlier the same day, the children of this family were threatened and called vulgar names. <u>Because of the acts of violence and harassment</u>, the family moved out the next morning. <u>The exploits</u> of a few empty-headed and bigoted individuals helped to move the <u>struggle for human rights</u> back one hundred years.

Conclusion

In conclusion, the fight for human rights is one that will continue until the end of time. Mankind has a hard time grasping the fact that we are all of the same mold. We are all humans, no matter what religion we practice, no matter what color we are, be it black, red, yellow, brown, or white. We all breathe, walk, talk, and have the same feelings. But until man realizes that to worship freely and to work and to live without discrimination are rights and not privileges, the fight for human rights will go on.

The Regents' essay topic "What is your most prized possession? Why?" gives the student the opportunity to respond in the first person "I." Any topic among the 493 can be developed using the first or third person, but the question with "you" in it particularly invites the "I" response. Cindy Montgomery succeeds in taking an abstract topic and filling it with specific details even in the introduction. It isn't just coffee—it's "Folger's Instant Coffee." She allows us to know something about her personality and her desire for independence as she tells us about her coffee cup collection. Again the structured opening is utilized as she introduces the three main ideas that she develops one by one in the body paragraphs; then she places a unifying thesis at the end of the introduction, making it the longest paragraph in the essay. The paper succeeds because of its tight organization and its original examples.

<u>"Coffee, Anyone?"</u>

CINDY MONTGOMERY
English 101H, Practice Regents' Exam
Topic: What is your most prized possession? Why?

Use of first person

Short narrative introduction before structured opening

1st idea

2nd idea

3rd idea

I MOVED OUT OF MY PARENTS' HOUSE AT THE AGE OF SEVENTEEN in search of my independence and freedom. I rented a small apartment, and on my first night there, I made myself a cup of Folger's Instant Coffee. I drank it out of the one and only coffee cup I owned. Somehow, drinking that coffee in my own kitchen, out of my own cup, seemed like the most grown-up thing I'd ever done. <u>After that experience, I began collecting coffee cups. I value my collection, and I still feel that same excitement about my independence when I use one of them. Many of them represent different facets of my personality through their different shapes, sizes, or designs. Over the years I've mentioned my collection to friends, and as a result I usually get a new cup when any of them travel to faraway places.</u>

Thesis	Collectively, I value my coffee cups probably more than anything else that I own.
1st idea developed	It may seem funny to someone else that my coffee cups represent freedom and independence to me. I guess the representation stems from asking for a drink of my parents' coffee when I was younger. The answer was inevitably, "No, coffee is for grown-ups." Needless to say, today I am an avid coffee drinker, and I have a choice of forty-eight different cups with which to express my grown-up taste.
2nd idea developed	I don't own a set of matching cups; each one is a different size, color, or shape. Each one of them expresses a piece of my personality. For example, I have a purple one, a grey one, and a pink one— my favorite colors. I am an animal lover, and I have cups with rabbits, cats, elephants, and turtles on them. I have a bad temper and a giant, fiery red coffee cup to prove it. Many of my cups express who I am and what I am like.
Most important point 3rd idea developed	Most important of all, my collection has been added to by special people in my life. My mother found a coffee cup store, and she has given me different cups over the years as gifts. Many of my friends travel overseas, and as a result I have cups from Israel, Amsterdam, Switzerland, France and Germany. When I use one of these cups, I not only think of the exotic place it came from but also of the very special person who gave it to me.
Summary of main points Repetition of answer to question Conclusion	I couldn't be paid enough to give up those friendships. I couldn't throw away myself or my independence, either. Likewise, I could never give away my coffee cups. The collection is a representation of me. It is something I can call my own, and <u>it is my most prized possession</u>.

Reading Cindy Montgomery's paper drawing on her personal experience brings up the point concerning the choice of topics. Which of the two test questions should the students choose when both are placed before them on the Regents' test booklet? The best answer is, "Write on the topic you feel closest to." The essayists get no extra points for writing on one topic rather than another—that is, they get no edge for writing on the topic outside their experience as opposed to the one inside their experience. Perhaps visualizing oneself inside the topic is the best technique to use, allowing the writer to judge if he/she has enough specific examples to develop the essay.

THE TWO PART THESIS WITH A SUBDIVISION

The essay on the Regents' topic: "Should sex education be taught in our public schools? Why or why not?" reveals a contrastive opening and a two-part Regents' thesis. Lindsey Malone then divides the issue of protection into two parts as she develops her essay and a natural unfolding effect occurs. The essay contains the usual clear topic sentences relating to the thesis and the specific detail so vital to satisfying the content requirement. The sharp divisions of the topic once more prevent the student from saying the same thing over and over again.

"Sex Education at an Early Age"

LINDSEY L. MALONE

English 101. Practice Regents' Essay

Topic: Should sex education be taught in our public schools?
Why or why not?

Contrastive
statements

Two-part thesis

SEX EDUCATION HAS BEEN A CONTROVERSIAL ISSUE FOR MANY years. Some people feel that it has no place in the classroom, and it should be kept at home. Other people feel that sex education should be taught in school but only to older children and only in vague impersonal terms. <u>Actually, sex education should be taught to children at the earliest age of comprehension, both at home and in school, because it is important to their psychological development and vital for their protection.</u>

1st part developed

Use of unifying
references,
phrases, and
possessive
adjectives (that,
this, these, their)
throughout essay

All children have a natural curiosity about sex, and this curiosity should be satisfied early with solid facts. Sex is something they whisper and giggle about, something no one talks about in front of them or discusses with them. <u>But</u> if adults do not explain sex to them, children have no way to <u>understand</u> it. <u>Not understanding</u> sex causes the child to fear it, and making it a taboo subject causes the child to develop negative connotations about it. So children come to think of sex as something frightening and dirty. It is unfortunate that children have to feel <u>that way</u> about something as wonderful as the reproductive process. Sex and the results of sex—children—are very positive and important things in our lives, and children should be let in on the "secret" at an early age.

[Transition]

2nd point
subdivided

Protection from outsiders is <u>another</u> vital reason to teach children about sex at an early age. Parents should explain to children what sex is for and when it is right. By telling a child that sex is for adults and by emphasizing that children are never to be involved in any type of sexual activity, the parent is giving his/her child knowledge he/she needs. <u>With this knowledge</u>, children can deter sexual advances made towards them, and they are able to report any such incidents because they understand what has happened and know that it is wrong. Children come in contact with possible child molesters every day through day care centers, schools, social activities, and sports. Sending a trusting and ignorant child up against these odds is like sending a lamb into a lion's den.

[Transition]

The strongest point

<u>Unfortunately</u>, children are often sexually abused in their own homes by the very family that should be caring for them. <u>These children</u> are often taught from an early age that the abuse they are suffering is a natural expression of family affection. <u>Their</u> only knowledge comes from the sick, manipulative, molesting relative. Sex education at an early age in schools could put a stop to this kind of sexual abuse. <u>By teaching the children the proper time and place for sex</u> and <u>by stressing that no one should be forcing them to engage in any form of sexual activity</u>, the schools can save a child years of

Major ideas
summarized

51

agony. The child has the knowledge to question what is happening to him/her and to report the abuse.

Children have a natural desire to know about the basic functions of their bodies. More importantly, they have a right to protect themselves from being sexually abused. By arming children with a thorough knowledge of sex, by teaching them at home and at school, we are giving them that right.

THE HUMOROUS/SATIRICAL DEVELOPMENT

A question often asked in the Regents' seminar is, "Should I try humor or satire when I write the Regents' essay?" The answer is if the writers succeed they will get rewarded for their original approach to a topic; they may even elicit a chuckle from the raters or at least bring a smile to their lips. But if the writers fail to entertain or to make a point, they certainly will be penalized for a feeble attempt at humor. Ken McCarley succeeds in his satirical approach to corporal punishment, but for most writers the advice would be to play it straight—especially with the time limitation of one hour.

"Let Us Crack Those Little Knuckles"

KEN McCARLEY
English 101, Argumentation-Satire
Practice Regents' Essay
Topic: "Children should be disciplined in the schools by corporal punishment."
Defend or attack this statement.

AT PRESENT THERE SEEMS TO BE SOME DEBATE WITH REGARD to the use of physical punishment in the classroom. For the sake of our children, a paddle should be readily handy in every teacher's drawer. Threats of, "I'll send you to the principal's office" or "You will get a demerit" are not effective with our youth. Instead, a few raps on the hand will whip the strayed children into line. As long as our teachers exercise some discretion with a "bolo paddle," many of the modern-day disciplinary problems facing our schools will be solved.

For too long, our young upstarts have badgered our teachers while basking in the light of a protective law that prohibits teachers from using a physical form of correction. They rest in the knowledge that they can sue any instructor who dares to lift even a finger against them. Teachers find themselves powerless against a disruptive youngster. The options available for discipline are limited. The teacher can yell, and in the process surrender some points to the child, or the teacher can pass the buck to the principal. Granted the trip to the principal's office is not pleasant (I have lost a few pounds myself through sweating as I waited for that ominous oaken door to swing open when the time came to enter), but a big man with a beer belly telling one to behave does not have the impact of a big wooden stick. The paddle is the answer.

Just the threat of being beaten would straighten out many a weak-kneed radical. Our teachers might put their paddles on display. A clever teacher could hang that paddle near the classroom's American flag so that in the morning, when the Pledge of Allegiance is recited, all those children with naughty plans for the day will reconsider, as their eyes focus not on "Old Glory" but on the dangling menace instead. Or, when a teacher senses that things are slipping from his authoritative grip, he can casually slap his stick against a nearby desktop. This will offer an auditory reminder of what lurks behind the next mischievous corner.

For those rebels without causes who do not adhere to the warnings, a swift smack will be in order. Students will quickly learn that stinging, swollen, reddened knuckles are not a fair price to pay for an ill-conceived prank. Their throbbing extremities will be a constant reminder. "Do not do that again; do not do that again; do not do that again." This "quick and dirty" form of punishment will certainly cause one to think twice before going astray again.

Remember the constraints of one hour.

This paper is not intended to advocate wholesale whipping of children. Teachers must not be "paddle happy." No parent would want to see a paddle in the hands of a teacher whose dog had just been hit by a truck or whose husband or wife had recently dashed off to Acapulco with a secret lover. Perhaps instructors could be "licensed to paddle" after being approved by a selected panel of sensible disciplinarians.

Those who succeed at using humor and satire will be rewarded; those who do not will be punished.

So, in order to correct society, in order to have children return to that "Leave It To Beaver" era, in order to make streets safe to walk on again, oak should meet skin in schools. With big sticks in the hands of level-headed teachers, we will surely see the return of the crew cut and the death of rock and roll.

THE CONTRASTIVE PARAGRAPH OR "ALTHOUGH CLAUSE" STRATEGY

Many students complain that they cannot divide the main idea into three parts as revealed in most of the models of the formulaic Regents' essay models. They jot down ideas, cluster them, and find that they have only two sharp divisions of the topic; then they panic because they do not have the required length. Several approaches to this problem might help allay their anxiety. Sometimes an extended example of one aspect of the thesis or an anecdote (a short narrative) might add just the original touch needed or at least the number of words required. Another solution is to jot down ideas on both sides of the argumentative topic chosen; there are always two sides or it would not be an argument—even some expository topics lend themselves to this technique. The writers select the side to write about concerning which they have the most evidence or ideas; usually the writers can develop two strong reasons for their stand. The other paragraph can simply be what others would say or the other point of view. Students should practice this contrasting idea popularly labeled as the "although clause" because in the Regents' preparation booklet for raters, it is praised as a superior, alternative approach. All raters read the handout as part of their training session prior to their evaluation of the essays. For eight years, I have been teaching the Regents' Preparation course to those who have failed the Regents' test twice and have polled my students after their taking of the exam as to their choice of thesis. The majority of writers who have practiced the technique choose the "although clause" to develop their topic because they think it is very helpful in organizing their ideas, finding it easier to list the opposition and then to develop two body paragraphs. Those students who have used this composition approach have a very high pass rate.

Therefore in choosing the topic concerning the government's subsidization of Olympic teams, Teri Kenith jotted down reasons for and against—deciding that the evidence and logic were stronger for government support. After she had clustered the topics, however, she realized that she could develop only two aspects—the insurance of a stronger and more talented Olympic team and the promotion of pride in our nation. She did have a jot list of ideas from her brainstorming of the pros and cons. She took those ideas against the support of the Olympics and developed them into a contrasting first paragraph, making sure that she had transitions between the list. The thesis contained the "although clause" to reveal to the rater her choice of development. The transitional sentence at the end of that contrasting body paragraph also made clear her stand on the issue.

"Support for Our Olympic Teams"

TERI KENITH
English 101, Practice Regents' Essay
Topic: "Should the government subsidize our Olympic teams?" Why or why not?

Narrative opening

WALKING THE STREETS AT THIS VERY MOMENT IS AN OLYMPIC star—not a current star, mind you, but a young man or woman who has the potential to become one of our brightest Olympic talents. Chances are, though, that this person will never do much more in life than grill hamburgers or press shirts at a dry cleaners, and the reason for this is pure and simple: money. Although there are many valid arguments against the government's financial support of our Olympic teams, subsidizing would help to insure a stronger and more talented team and would also help to promote pride in our nation.

Use of "although" clause

Contrastive paragraph listing reasons against, transitions between to bind 2nd paragraph

Certainly, there are many valid arguments against the government's subsidizing the Olympics. Opponents argue that there are millions of people in the United States living below the poverty line. They argue that we need to build a strong defense and that there are already too many free hand-outs. The four trillion dollar federal deficit is another point of the opposition. With that debt hanging over our heads, who needs to spend more? Of course, the rising and seemingly uncontrollable crime rate is another protest. Many feel that improved law enforcement and modern prisons should be the

54

nation's number one priority. <u>These are all valid negative aspects of spending more on the Olympics, but the positive arguments far outweigh the negative.</u>

<u>If we did subsidize the Olympic teams, we would have stronger and more talented teams.</u> <u>Those</u> talented young people who aren't able to train properly because of lack of funding would be able to train and perfect their talents. Russia's athletes receive paid training during their whole athletic career and it shows. They always seem to earn more medals than any other country. <u>Also</u>, if the government subsidized the teams, we might have larger and more versatile teams. In case one star athlete were injured, another could take his place.

<u>Our pride in our nation's performance is also sorely lacking.</u> As well as our teams do now, think of the added pride <u>our</u> nation would be feeling if we did even better. With more and better trained athletes, we are bound to fare even better in the competition. <u>This</u> increased pride that America would be feeing would allow us to project confidence to the rest of the world. The world might <u>then</u> accord us the respect that we have somehow lost. Winning in international competition gives us and other nations the feeling that <u>our</u> form of government promotes excellence. <u>Moreover</u>, competing successfully on the playing field might obviate the need for building bigger and better missiles to prove <u>our</u> national prowess.

The Olympic teams are our source of pride and accomplishment, and we should encourage their success by whatever means is available. They are our showcase to the rest of the world. They are a peaceful way to project what America is all about—freedom and excellence.

THE NARRATIVE OPTION

The narrative and descriptive techniques are used less often in developing an entire Regents' essay, but they can be invaluable in adding specific details or examples in developmental paragraphs. However sometimes a whole essay can be fleshed-out with a story or sensual imagery. The following Regents' essays are detailed in a specific, unified, coherent, original manner by utilizing narrative and descriptive development.

WRITE ABOUT
SOMETHING YOU
DO OR
SOMETHING YOU
KNOW ABOUT.

WRITING CAN EXPRESS
AN IDEA AND/OR AN
EMOTION; IT EXPRESSES
YOU

"A Nose With Character"

WENDY GOODWIN
English 101, Timed Regents' Test
Topic: Do you think heredity or environment has had a greater effect upon what you are? Explain.

<table>
<tr><td>Descriptive opening</td><td></td></tr>
</table>

I AM FIVE FEET, SEVEN INCHES TALL. I HAVE BLUE EYES, blonde hair, and a nose with character. All the above are physical attributes that the world sees first and say, "This is Wendy." Although heredity pre-determined what I was to look like through this meeting of the "x" and "y" chromosomes, its importance stops there. My early environment, interacting with an alcoholic, dysfunctional parent, has had the greatest effect on my becoming what I am—a responsible adult and a loving, understanding human being.

Regents' topic developed by narrative

Thesis

My earliest memories of my childhood were not unlike most others. I was a happy child. My family was loving, and my dad was "Superman." That nurturing environment began to change when I was about seven years old. My dad seldom came home, and when he did, he was abusive, withdrawn, and drunk. I wasn't aware that I was learning how I was to deal with life later on by being exposed to my father's solution, "the bottle." Dad made this choice to avoid feeling, his inadequacy, guilt, and anger. Given this environment, I too began to avoid my feelings. What I wanted most as an adolescent was for my father to love me the way he used to; I wanted to curl up in his lap and have him tell me everything was going to be all right and that his little girl was safe; Daddy was there. These are healthy thoughts and feelings for a child of seven but not for a child of twenty-six which is what I was, a very needy child inside an over-responsible adult's body.

Narrative of childhood and adolescence

Without my early environment, I would not have found the many wonderful support systems and people who have become important to my growth and development. I began to see the need for help in dealing with my father's alcoholism; I felt angry, fearful, and inadequate most of the time. I knew I did not have to feel this way. But I didn't know how else to feel. I began looking for help and found "Adult Children of Alcoholics," a group of adults all having one or more alcoholic parents. It has been through this group's love and support that I have been able to free my parents of the responsibility of taking care of the child within me, and I have been able to assume that powerful role in my own life. Without this group's help, I don't think I would have been able to discover what tremendous freedom comes with accepting responsibility for the choices I've made in my life. I've been able to replace the picture of my curling up in Dad's lap with my walking straight and tall, holding his hand as we grow together.

Topic sentence

Unifying references

Combination of narrative and expository

It has been through my struggle to overcome the alcoholic surroundings of my early years that I now am able to be so understanding and tolerant of what others are going through and their

Analysis

56

need for love and support. I want to be there when others need me because they were there in my times of distress.

Conclusion

Restatement of thesis

Heredity has determined what I look like, but my environment has given me a message of life, love, growth, and understanding to share with others. My interaction with an alcoholic parent and my effort to understand it has had the greatest impact on what I am today. I am a wonderful surprise!

THE DESCRIPTIVE STRATEGY

ETHELYN H. SLAVIN
Regents' Essay
Topic: "Which of the four seasons of the year
appeals to you the most? Why?

Listing development in opening

EACH SEASON OF THE YEAR HAS SOMETHING SPECIAL TO OFFER. Summer blows sultry heat night and day. Frosty winter makes our eyes water while we huddle around a friendly fire. Lovely spring is alive with promises of flowers budding and birds nesting. But autumn is the season that appeals to me the most because it has the magic of unpredictable temperature, breathtaking beauty, and the promise of holidays to come.

3-part thesis

Topic sentence

1st part developed

Use of sense of touch

Think of the magical way that Indian summer creeps into the chilly days of autumn. Just when we feel certain that we'll be able to wear our new sweaters, the temperature rises to foil us. We put the sweaters back in the drawer. Sure enough, the next day is crisp as lettuce, just right for a woolly wrap. Autumn can really fool us that way.

Topic sentence

2nd part developed

Use of sense of sight

One way it does not try to fool us is with its incredible beauty. Every multi-colored leaf is a genuine product of nature. The vibrant reds and golds melt into each other on the trees, until the trees become a forest of fantastic display. Leaves are everywhere, overhead and underfoot. Late-blooming "firecrackers" burst forth on the lawn showing yet another shade of red from autumn's palette. And the fall harvest of apples, pears, pumpkins, and more proves that bounty exists even in this late season.

Topic sentence

3rd part developed

Time line

As the pumpkins appear in our Hallowe'en decor, we begin to realize that Thanksgiving is not far away. We look forward to a gathering of family and friends and a meal that will make our buttons pop. There is much shopping to do and so many plans to make. And we know that after Thanksgiving we will begin to anticipate Christmas and then a new year. The season holds such promises out to us, and we embrace them.

Simile
Conclusion
Personification
Poetic imagery

Autumn, then is <u>much like an unpredictable woman</u>; we don't know exactly what to expect from her. But in time she unfolds all of her beauty, charm, and wit. It is difficult not to be seduced by autumn's magic, and even more difficult not to fall in love with her.

The Regents' test models published in <u>The Polishing Cloth</u> make public an issue of assessment of college level writing in the state of Georgia. The students find out through the essays what the expectations are in the 60-minute essay test. They can also see that there is a variety of ways to pass the test, and that realization takes the mystery and anxiety out of the rating process. The increase in the sales of the magazine as the students prepare for the Regents' test indicates that the publication empowers the students to take charge of their own learning. <u>The Polishing Cloth</u> sold in DeKalb College bookstores is a powerful tool for students helping other students to pass the Regents' essay examination.

PART V
ALTERNATE APPROACHES IN COMPOSITION

THE NARRATIVE APPROACH

When your RTP or English instructor tells you that it is wise to adjust your writing style to the Regents' topic assigned, there are definitions of types of composition that may help you to understand where and how to start. The more options you have to develop a topic, the more control you will feel as a writer. Therefore, your knowledge of these various modes or ways of composing should not make you more inflexible or narrow as an author but should allow you to see that it is these approaches or their combinations that give you the length and variety needed to develop your topic. Knowledge is power—the more power you have as a writer, the less stress you will experience in taking the Regents' essay test. You are not trapped in a formulaic approach to composition; the door is open.

Let's start with the definition of the narrative. I often tell my students that the narrative approach is the most simple mode of composing because even a child can tell a story, but it also can be the most complex as the great authors of the world manipulate it and complicate it with themes and variations. As a student who is going to take the Regents' essay test, you need to know that this narrative approach is not only acceptable but "meritorious"—a favorite Regents' term.

Definition of the Narrative Essay

Much of the writing that you do is devoted to telling what happened. This is narrative or story writing, and you divide it into paragraphs to make it clear and interesting to the reader. A narrative paragraph, however, does not need to be so carefully constructed as paragraphs in other kinds of writing. It is not always possible to have a topic sentence in every paragraph when you are relating an experience or telling a story. You change paragraphs when the action of your story shifts to a different scene, when you bring in a new character, when you wish to insert a descriptive passage, or when you change to a different time.

A narrative essay is almost always written in chronological order because, by its very nature, a story moves in time order in which its events happen. The following words are commonly used in narrative writing to make the order of events clear: first, second, third, finally, next, hence, therefore, consequently, as a result, meanwhile, at length, immediately, soon, afterward, after a few days, in the meantime, later, now.

Other suggestions: For a Regents' essay make sure a thesis is present in the opening paragraph. Select a story worth writing about and one that ties in with and illustrates the topic. Use first person. Compose a conclusion that answers the Regents' question.

Every quarter I have students complain that they have no stories to tell to flesh out the Regents' topics. I don't believe them, and if you are feeling the same way, I don't believe you. Convince yourself that you are an interesting person because you are. You just need to be aware of what you and those around you are doing and saying. These incidents become the substance of your narrative essays.

SIX POINTS FOR SUCCESS

Since the earliest times, the story has captured our attention. Even today the television, which is watched six and one-half to seven hours daily by the average person, is a storytelling medium. Think about the raters of your essay sitting in a conference room or classroom on a Saturday morning, reading essay after essay. Imagine those graders being able to sink themselves, however briefly, into a story—whether it be in the introduction, one body paragraph, or the entire essay. These raters can enter your world and be entertained by your ideas. Certainly it is helpful if the topic lends itself to narrative development, but if you leave yourself open to that possibility your control as a writer is enhanced. <u>Here are six points that will help you be successful:</u>

1. Be confident that you are an interesting person. Even some of our great writers keep telling the same story over and over with different variations.

2. Make meaning out of your life by analyzing your life stories. Even painful memories help you to make order out of chaos.

3. Because you know a story from your life or those close to you, your thoughts will flow easily. They will be organized quickly and naturally into a time order.

4. Answer the question of the Regents' topic early in the introduction—in the first sentence if possible. Make sure that you have a thesis. But it can and should be a very simple one.

5. Control the story. Don't let it take over. Make it work for you by answering the topic question.

6. Make sure that you have a conclusion that restates the thesis and ties in the story with the topic.

Regents' Essays Developed by Narration

The following essays show the above average (3) or superior results (4) from developing the Regents' topic with the narrative. See how the essay flows as it is naturally organized by the time line.

The "LIVING WILL" DIRECTS A PERSON'S FAMILY AND PHYSICIANS NOT TO KEEP THAT PERSON ALIVE BY ARTIFICIAL MEANS IF THAT PERSON WERE TO SUFFER A TOTALLY INCAPACITATING DISEASE OR ILLNESS. WOULD YOU CONSIDER SIGNING SUCH A DOCUMENT AND GIVING IT TO YOUR OWN FAMILY? WHY OR WHY NOT?

Entire essay developed by narrative	<u>Beyond a shadow of doubt I would sign a "Living Will" document and give it to my parents.</u> I have very strong feelings for this issue based upon personal experiences. <u>To me the choice is an easy one that I made several years ago because of an incident that involved by best friend.</u>	Answers the question Simple thesis
Time line	Four years ago there was a terrible car wreck that took place in a small town in Southeast Georgia. On a rainy day two kids were out joy riding when their car skidded beneath a tractor trailer rig. The impact killed the driver instantly and sent the passenger at the age of seventeen into a coma.	Story of a wreck
Time line	When I went to the hospital with my best friend, we saw her brother hooked up to some kind	Personal involvement with passenger after wreck

61

of machine that had tubes running everywhere. There were some in his nose, some on his arms, and there were even a few in his legs. My friend and I stood there for hours staring in disbelief, sometimes crying and sometimes trying to laugh.

Time line

It has been almost five years since that horrible day but none of us are over the shock of it. For my friend's brother is still hooked up to that cold machine and he always will be. Some vital organs had been smashed, and he cannot function on his own. He will never speak to any of us or hear or see us. I have watched that family suffer more than any one family ever deserves to. I have witnessed their daily visits turn into weekly ones and their weekly ones into monthly ones. All this family wants is for their son and loved one to die so that he may go to heaven.

Continuing pain over time for narrator and for family

Based upon this personal experience it is an easy choice for me to sign the "Living Will" document and give it to my family. For I would never want them to have to suffer every day like my friend's family. I would much rather my family remember me as a human being as opposed to a vegetable.

Rating: 3

SHOULD COLLEGE STUDENTS BE REQUIRED TO TAKE PHYSICAL EDUCATION COURSES? WHY OR WHY NOT?

One day in the life of—

For the average college student, formal physical education courses may prove to be too much of a good thing. Oh no, I'm not knocking physical fitness, but for sheer physical endurance both required and acquired, consider one day the life of a commuting college student—me.

Answers the question— qualifying statement— Simple thesis

Time line from waking up to boarding the Marta train

Rolling out of bed is my first warm-up exercise. At the breakfast table, I exercise great restraint— no butter, dry toast. I stretch my imagination as I creatively pair yet another T-shirt with my old reliable jeans. Having given my teeth a brush and a promise, I leap into my Honda Civic and race to the Kiss-Ride parking lot. With amazing dexterity I run up a down escalator, fingers clutching a moist little pile of coins. With incredible manual dexterity I manage to exert sufficient force to move the turnstile one notch. With moments to spare, I leap onto the platform, and from there into the train. Once in

Specific details on exercise

my seat, the now demure Pavlova, I enjoy my ten minute break.

ballet dancer

Time line from train ride into the classroom

The trip from train into classroom is much the same—same muscles, same exercises, same inherent obstacles. The classroom, however, offers exercise of a different sort. There are certain core curriculum courses which, if allowed the full power of their existence, will bore one to extinction. One must exercise great restraint in such a situation. Then, of course, we have the intense isotonic exercise for the buttocks of sitting on them, relieved only by the occasional squirm for a two hour lecture on "The Curiously Erotic Art of Chinese Footbinding." (I love these new ethnic studies!) And no class would be complete without having to cope with a full bladder and an absolute necessity to take furious and copious notes. My sphincter muscle has acquired a tone here-to-fore only written up in the medical literature.

Humorous seated exercises

Time line back to Marta train ride

I now have only to sprint back to the transit station to qualify for a Presidential Sports Award. Woe be unto the unsuspecting mugger who attempts to mug my mug, for I am poised, ready and aware. My bulging eyeballs rotate quickly in a muscular peripheral sweep of the station. Anyone who dares to monkey with my inner city paranoia risks a sound thrashing. I don't usually brag, but my umbrella thwack got me into the Olympic trials. Test me if you dare.

The exercises associated with commuter's perils

So, you see, physical fitness is already inherent in the commuting college student. From home to train to class and back again, a person must be in shape. I've got the biceps to prove it.

The conclusion ties in with topic and thesis.

Rating: 4

HAVE YOUR EATING HABITS CHANGED SINCE YOU'VE BEEN IN COLLEGE? DISCUSS.

Contextual

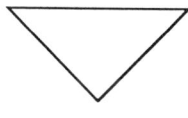

opening—Broad ideas narrowed to a thesis

College can help to bring about many changes in an individual. Intellectual changes, perceptual changes, and even changes in personal habits may all play a role in the college experience. The area of personal eating habits is perhaps one of the most commonly discussed changes observed in college freshmen. The concept of the "Freshman fifteen," referring to the tendency of college freshmen to gain weight, has proven itself no myth in my own experience.

Simple thesis

When I began college, I had generally healthy eating habits, a product of having lived with my parents all my life and being forced to eat my vegetables. In my first four months of college life, I tried to continue these habits which had been ingrained in me since the early days of <u>strained spinach;</u> however, as the freedoms of college became more apparent, I realized that I did not have to finish my <u>green beans</u> in order to have <u>chocolate cake</u>. I seemed to come to this decision simultaneously with the rest of the girls in my freshman dorm. Soon the lobby of our building became a receiving line for the <u>Domino's Pizza</u> delivery man. This trend continued as evidenced by the <u>boxes of candy</u> and <u>bags of potato chips</u> lined up across our desks that gave a whole new meaning to the term "cramming." By the end of my freshman year I had gained close to twenty-five pounds. Two main factors made this transformation take place so smoothly that I never even noticed it happening: the fact that everyone else did the same thing and the absolute absence of any type of measuring device such as a simple bathroom scale.

<u>Fortunately, since my first year at an institute of higher learning, I have learned that I will have to take responsibility for my own eating habits.</u> I now know that my mother will no longer watch over my shoulder to make sure I have eaten my carrots instead of slipping them to the dog; I will have to do that job for her. I have also discovered that chocolate cake can be a wonderful thing when taken in moderation, but when eaten in excess, it becomes the nemesis of my hips. I have also realized that when I eat better, I feel better, and I perform better.

Rating: 3

WHAT IS YOUR MOST PRIZED POSSESSION? WHY?

<u>My most prized possession is a memory.</u> Once I had a dream, a goal in life that consumed all my waking hours. That dream was bitterly stolen from me. It disappeared in a few tragic moments on a icy highway, leaving my life forever changed.

I was once a dancer, twirling to "Heartbreak Hotel" when I was three years old. I had a knack for being able to feel the music, to become the music, my parents tell me. At age five, I enrolled in pre-ballet courses and continued until I was eight.

Margin notes: Time line / Specific details / We eat the food with her. / Analysis / Narrative examples / Raters like to see that writers learn from events in their lives / Answers the question / Simple thesis

At that time my teachers felt that they could no longer teach me, for they realized that I had exceptional potential. By the time I was twelve, I was training with a company in Chicago. My first major role came to me that year, Clara in *The Nutcracker*. Of course, it was that one, for most ballerinas make their professional debut as Clara or the Sugar-plum Fairy in *The Nutcracker*.

> Details easily organized by narrative form.

When I was fourteen, I transferred to a school in New York and became a member of the Academy of Arts. There I met the legendary Misha and hoped that someday I would be lucky enough to work with him. My extension was almost perfect, and I seemed to have everything going for me. I worked hard and spent all of my time in the studio or on the stage. I was at the Academy until I was sixteen. It never occurred to me that my world was extremely limited and that I had almost no knowledge of how to function in the real world, the "secular" world. I came face to face with this realization one night in 1985.

> Time line

> Specific details

> Analysis

I was going to Indiana to be with my family for Christmas. Patrick, a friend of mine, was driving. Sleet was coming down fast, forming a thin sheet of ice on the road. Suddenly a semi-truck hit us, slicing the "Patmobile" almost in half. I suffered severe trauma to my head, broke my legs in three places, and messed up my equilibrium. Patrick lost both his legs and became so despondent that he killed himself six months later. I found that the damage to my sense of balance completely destroyed my ability to dance, so my career was over. I tried to find a new life for myself by becoming involved in radio and television broadcasting and production. Now that is my major.

> Time line

> Analysis

This may sound like a depressing life story, but the memory of my dancing years far outweighs the pain of losing them. The innocence of that time and the joy I found in learning to turn ballet into poetry is a beautiful thing that will always move me to tears. I don't feel that I live in the past. When I think of those precious moments, they give me the hope and inspiration to be the best that I can be—now—today.

> Analysis

> The student makes sense out of her painful experience.

Rating: 3

Narrative Introductions

In addition to the ease of organizing narrative essays, the students often find that narrative introductions bring them quickly into the thesis as they visualize themselves in the topic assigned. One of my students always had difficulty with repetitive, empty introductions until one day when writing about a Regents' topic on mass transit or public transportation, he told about waiting in the Marta station on a rainy day and feeling the relief of being able to travel easily and economically and safely to his destination. After that story-line introduction, he broke through the dull, wooden barrier of his opening sentences and went on to write introduction after introduction through seeing himself in the topic provided. Sometimes as with the entire narrative essay, the memory can be painful. But again pain often brings insight as revealed in Gwen Ashby's essay on the causes of teen suicide:

Descriptive details

Narrative opening

> He is 5'7" tall, and he weighs 96 pounds. He has a poor appetite, has trouble sleeping, is withdrawn . . . all classic symptoms of depression. When I visit him, he rarely smiles, sometimes cries, and answers my questions in a flat monotone voice. He is 13, and he is my son. He has been diagnosed as having a Major Depressive Episode. I have watched Ronnie go steadily downhill since his father and I divorced seven years ago. Ronnie never adjusted to the break-up of his family, to having a father who lived all the way across the country, a father he rarely saw or heard from. Ronnie doesn't like living in a hospital, but he wasn't happy at home, and doctors warned that he was suicidal. There are other teenagers on the adolescent unit at the hospital who are suffering from depression. Many of them have already attempted suicide, and the majority of these young people come from broken homes. <u>Although drugs and other pressures contribute to the rising rate of teenage suicide, the increase in divorce probably is the main cause of adolescents' killing themselves in record numbers today</u>.

graphic specific details leading naturally to thesis

Thesis using although clause

Extended Examples

<u>Extended examples</u> which help supply the needed length of a Regents' essay can also be developed into paragraphs to support the thesis. In one RTP class a student who needed a body paragraph to support his stand on gun control told the story of a little boy opening the glove compartment of a car and finding a gun and then shooting his sister. Another essayist used the extended example as a vital paragraph to explain the epidemic of school drop-outs as she let us see the dilemma of a pregnant teenager who sat alone in her bedroom struggling with her despair. Paul Kelly not only found the narrative valuable in introducing his topic—"Do you favor or oppose a rule that would prohibit professional teams from recruiting college athletes until their college sports eligibility is over? Why or why not?"—but also used an extended narrative example to allow the reader to feel the plight of the college athlete:

> <u>Introduction:</u> In 1972 Spencer Hayward of the University of California in Los Angeles (UCLA) left college after his junior year and after participating in the 1972 Summer Olympics in Munich to pur-

sue a career with the New York Knicks of the National Basketball Association (NBA). The United States Supreme Court ruled, over the objections of UCLA officials, to grant Hayward "hardship eligibility," or the right to earn a salary as a professional basketball payer. Since 1972 hundreds of student athletes have left school early to earn the massive salaries professional sports offer. Because they sacrifice their college eligibility and thus their college education, they also risk any future aside from sports. If they do not succeed, they will ultimately be doing menial labor for a small wage. Those factors violate the integrity of amateur athletics, undermine the university's efforts to educate, and potentially harm the student athlete who is often left with no education and not a great deal of hope for the future. <u>Therefore, a rule prohibiting professional teams from recruiting non-eligible players should be instituted</u>.

Extended example (later on in same essay)

A good look at the student athlete's well being should also be considered. The case of Walter "Stinky" Daniels is a sad one. "Stinky" came out of Macon, Georgia, to the University of Georgia as one of the hottest basketball recruits in the nation. After two years at Georgia, Daniels gave in to the lure of the money and signed a contract with the NBA's New Orleans (now Utah) Jazz. After one dismal season, Daniels was released from the team and was last seen doing custodial work at a central Georgia high school. He has no education, little money, and even less hope. Had he not been allowed to leave school early, he might have completed his education. A degree would have at least allowed him the opportunity to find gainful employment aside from basketball. It is a sad case, indeed.

In another Regents' essay rated 4, the author uses extended examples to illustrate her major points about the qualifications of a person who wishes to be a leader. She uses specific details to develop a three paragraph essay about Marlene Rubenstein.

ANALYZE THE QUALIFICATIONS IN A PERSON WHO WISHES TO BE A LEADER

Marlene Rubenstein would lose a beauty contest to an army boot. With her flat nose and thick glasses, she was the ugliest member of my high school class, including the goat used as team mascot. But Marlene was chosen president during her sophomore, junior, and senior years; and in college she led student government for three years. Marlene's success is not a mystery: she wins because she possesses the qualities of a good leader. Although many qualities contribute to leadership, Marlene's major assets are her ability to accept responsibility and her resourcefulness.

Accepting responsibility means being able to carry a project through to completion. In the tenth grade, Harvey Williams, the boy in charge of the Sophomore Class Float, had an appendectomy. Marlene took over as float chairman. She organized two teams of workers to build frames after school and divided the whole class into three groups who took turns on weekends. We completed the float four days ahead of schedule and had plenty of time to make changes in the final form. As a result we won First Place. What I didn't know at the time was that Marlene had promised Mr. Stevens, the chemistry teacher, that she would build a Vandegraf generator for the science fair. I later discovered that Marlene got up each morning at 6:00 to work on her science project. Needless to say, she also won first place in the fair competition.

In addition to accepting responsibility and completing the obligations required, Marlene could always be counted on to solve problems through her resourcefulness. For example, when the paper mache walls on our tenth grade float fell over, Marlene had us dip pillow cases in wet flour and hang them on ropes stretched horizontally between the wooden pillars. This gave us a perfect textured wall! Just before the parade, we discovered a flat tire on the float wagon. Marlene immediately turned a wheelbarrow upside down as a fulcrum and had three boys use an extra four by four as a Jack while two of the others quickly changed tires! Marlene's resourcefulness, like her willingness to accept responsibility, made us respect her and want her as a leader. It is not surprising that Marlene is now running for the U.S. Senate.

It is clear that the narrative has its place in helping you to develop your Regents' topic. As Ann Berthoff, author and teacher, remarks, "We don't take in the world like a camera or a set of recording devices. The mind is an agent, not a passive receiver. . . . The active mind is a composer and everything we respond to, we compose." Develop an active mind; keep your eyes open; your stories are waiting to be told.

THE DESCRIPTIVE APPROACH

There is truly a fine line between <u>description</u> and <u>narration</u> to such an extent that the writer often blends the two techniques, creating a descriptive incident. The two modes complement and enhance each other as authors give enough details and sensory images to allow readers to recreate the incident in their minds—to visualize it. Both approaches are easy to use because they are based on experiences that are very close to the writers. These images and details are based on first hand knowledge. But what separates the two approaches—narrative and descriptive—is the emphasis on the direct appeal to the senses that makes us taste, touch, see, feel, and hear what is going on around us in the descriptive essay. A further distinction is the focus on action in the narrative as opposed to the descriptive technique of observation. The writers of description either survey the scene from one vantage point, creating a dominant impression, or they take us from place to place in a spatial pattern of organization.

What does this alternate approach, description, mean to you as you attempt to find the most effective way to develop a Regents' topic? Let us begin with an explanation of the descriptive essay:

Definition of the Descriptive Essay

Descriptive writing is usually developed by a means of descriptive facts which together make-up the picture you are trying to describe. To make the readers feel as if they are in the scene described, you should appeal to the five senses—hearing, sight, taste, smell, and touch.

The order of details

When you have planned what you want to include in the essay by jotting down a list of ideas, then you must decide in what order you will record the various details. The natural order in a descriptive essay is the order in which the parts of the picture appeared to you. You may, of course, for the sake of clearness, describe the scene from left to right, foreground to background, or top to bottom. On the other hand, you may go from picture to picture in whatever order you think is most effective, provided you are keeping the reader informed as to where you are going. The use of connecting words and phrases will help the reader follow you.

The use of connectives or transitional expressions

The following words and phrases will prove useful in making clear to the reader the location of each point you are describing: here, beyond, on my left, on my right, nearby, opposite to, adjacent to, on the opposite side, in the distance, above, and below.

Other suggestions

For a Regents' essay, make sure a thesis is present in the opening paragraph. Provide sharp divisions of that thesis. Use first or third person. Avoid superlatives such as "beautiful" and "wonderful" and concentrate on precise sensory details to create your picture.

Topics Inviting Descriptive Development

How can you tell if you should utilize the descriptive approach in a Regents' essay? More than in any other type of essay development, the use of description is dictated or at least strongly suggested by the topic assigned. Consider the topics "Which of the four seasons of the year appeals to you the most? Why?" or "What is your favorite holiday? Why?" These topics demand that you include the appeal to the senses as you create your word pictures. Other topics that may use in-depth sensory detail often combined with stories and followed by explanation and analysis are the following:

1. What type of music do you prefer? Why?

2. Given the choice would you rather live in the mountains or near the beach? Discuss.

3. Name some place you would not like to go on a date and explain why you would choose not to go there.

4. How can Halloween be made safer for young people?

5. What region of the United States do you like most? Why?

6. Is there one place on earth that means more to you than all the others? Why?

7. Would you prefer to rear a family in the city or the country? Explain why.

8. Discuss what you like or do not like about the South.

9. America has many regional foods. What would you recommend to a traveller who would like to experience Southern food? Explain.

10. What is your most prized possession?

11. What is the value of foreign travel?

12. What is your favorite piece of furniture? Why?

13. What is your idea of a perfect vacation? Why?

14. Explain why you do not like having picnics.

15. What foreign country would you like to visit and why would you like to go there?

16. If you were to set up a personal museum of the most significant objects you own, what would you include and why?

If you would choose any of these topics, you would find that although description may be the dominant form of development, it is its combination with exposition that allows you to write the length of essay required. One topic that uses description primarily but also employs comparison and contrast is illustrated by two Regents' essays—one practice and one actual, rated 4.

Regents' Essays Developed by Description

Practice Regents' Essay

TOPIC: WHEN WE RETURN TO PLACES WE KNEW AS CHILDREN, WE ARE OFTEN SURPRISED AT HOW DIFFERENT THESE PLACES SEEM. COMPARE AND/OR CONTRAST YOUR IMPRESSIONS OF SOME PLACE YOU KNEW AS A CHILD WITH YOUR CURRENT IMPRESSION OF THE SAME PLACE.

Descriptive details—structured past

present

My aunt Mildred's house was a wonderful playground for me as a child. The spacious rooms that were generously endowed with interesting hiding places, the bedrooms that sported handmade quilts and real feather pillows, and, most importantly, the gardens where I was "princess" over a beautiful kingdom, all these hold countless memories for me. However, upon returning several years later, I discovered my playground had changed. Everything seemed cramped. The bed overwhelmed the bedroom, and the gardens appeared to be only a tangle of ugly, twisted weeds. My private park, as well as my childhood, seemed to have withered to the reality of maturity.

Writer chooses a place she knows well.

Contrast

thesis

Senses of smell and taste

Explaining by relating to something different

When my childhood fantasies continued to run rampant, the rooms of the house were wonderful. The warm kitchen always smelled of cookies, and there seemed to be an endless supply of lemonade. Just being in the room cheered my heart out of every seemingly irresoluble problem. However, as the years passed, something changed. Was it the house? Had it lost its magic? As I walked around the rooms, the changes were so depressingly evident. The kitchen that had once been so airy and carefree felt dingy and burdened by age. The kitchen smelled different too. It how held the smell of age, the scent one recognizes as a hospital odor.

Past

transition to present contrast (block structure)

Senses of sight and touch

Hoping to find the rest of my fantasy world still the same, I walked on through the house to the bedroom. The bed that had engulfed me as a child seemed to be an average bed, yet it still seemed to hold all the space in the room. Where was the bed that used to be there? These dull, flat quilts couldn't be the magnificent, fluffy quilts that covered me as a girl!

past

present (block structure)

Sight

touch

sight

touch and hearing combined

Calmly, I walked to the gardens to see if my kingdom was as beautiful as it once had been. The once lovely crepe myrtles weren't as pink as they once had been. The grass didn't feel soft enough to roll on, sleep on, or sit on. It felt stiff and appeared slightly gray instead of the brilliant emerald it had once been. The oak tree that once had been the most immense object in the garden appeared gnarled and twisted. The flowers I once had braided into wonderful crowns were gone. Instead, there were brittle, brown stalks, and weeds had taken over, strangling the life from the flowers.

Sentence by sentence contrast (side by side contrast)

Writer feels strong emotional loss.

I felt crushed. My dream world as a child had been lost to reality. I was forced to understand. To become an adult, I had given up a wild and colorful fantasy world in exchange for my maturity. My sense of loss was great as I realized that time had taken a beautifully imaginative little girl and slowly turned that girl into what is now an adult, a conservative, aging woman who can only dare to dream of the return of her long-gone individuality and joie de vivre.

Analysis—sentence by sentence contrast

Actual Regents' Essay, Rated 4

TOPIC: WHEN WE RETURN TO PLACES WE KNEW AS CHILDREN WE ARE OFTEN SURPRISED AT HOW DIFFERENT THESE PLACES SEEM. COMPARE AND/OR CONTRAST YOUR IMPRESSION OF SOME PLACE YOU KNEW AS A CHILD WITH YOUR CURRENT IMPRESSION OF THE SAME PLACE.

Time line

Sight and smell

Dialogue (hearing touch)

The place I knew and loved the most when I was young was my grandparents' house. Shortly after I was born, my parents were separated, and for the first five years of my life, my grandparents' house was my home. It was a wondrous place within due to nature. Poppa was a man of great kindness, wisdom and humor. My mother was working during these years, so my grandmother was the primary caregiver to my sister and me. We thought of Granny with the same bond that one has for one's mother. The house was full of love and warmth. Granny and Pop's yard was very large, and we watched the trees grow that Poppa had planted and saw hundreds of flowers bloom in Granny's flower islands all over the backyard. There was a rose arbor with benches underneath. A creek ran along behind the property, and Pop used to tell his friends, "I haven't had a grandchild yet who hasn't fallen in the creek." We spent many hours wading in there and tossing stones. Next

Writer knows place well.

emotional ties

Appeal to senses intermingled naturally.

door was a wooded lot into which opened a large drainpipe that ran under the pitted dirt road their house was on. Many more hours were spent there with imaginations running wild, games being invented, and friends secure and alone listening to the occasional car traveling overhead. It was a haven, a sanctuary. It was Granny and Poppa's house.

hearing

Although we moved away when I was five, my grandparents remained there until I was grown. It was a place for the family to return to again and again. When they sold their house, my sister and brother and I felt as if we had lost a friend, but to our surprise the grief was short lived. The love, the warmth and security we felt there, traveled with them to their new home. Being with them had the same wondrous aura as always, and we found that we soon forgot about their first house.

Time line

Past comparison

Returning to the old neighborhood several years ago, I was surprised as I sat in the street and looked at their house. The street was now concrete, and the cars whizzed by as I looked in awe at how small the yard had grown. The trees were still as beautiful as before but gone were the rows and rows of brilliant flowers that knew Gran's touch. The vacant lots were now peppered with new modern houses, and our drain pipe opened into someone's front yard. Our roaming areas in the neighborhood were all but gone, and there were children everywhere instead of the handful that had been my friends. I thought to myself that it was gone for good, that special place with its now shrunken yard, my haven lost forever. But then, I thought that was all right because my memories will be a part of me forever, and the people who made that place so special had a hand in forming my soul.

present

sensory details

Side by side contrast

Coming to terms with reality

analysis

Of course the descriptive technique is often used in <u>introductions</u>, as <u>one body paragraph</u>, or as an <u>extended example</u>. Again, having the freedom to employ these different modes and knowing how to enhance your writing by opening the door to all forms of expression should help you feel empowered as a writer. Note the variety of ways description can be used to develop your Regents' essay.

Descriptive introduction

Actual Regents' Essay, Rated 3

Attention-getting details

TOPIC: EXPLAIN WHY YOU DO OR DO NOT HUNT.

A person can always tell when it is hunting season. The air is crisp, and the smell of earth and blood is in the air. From out of nowhere come a multitude of pickup trucks and four wheel drives with gun racks and dead animals tied to the hoods of their cars as bloody trophies. Orange caps and jackets and dead bodies mark the return of the hunters. Yes, indeed, this is what hunting means to me. I do not hunt because I find it extremely repulsive.

Appeal to senses

Simple thesis

Use of description in one body paragraph after a narrative introduction

Actual Regents' Essay, Rated 4

TOPIC: IF YOUR DOCTOR TOLD YOU THAT YOU HAD ONLY A FEW MONTHS TO LIVE, HOW WOULD YOU ALTER YOUR WAY OF LIFE? DISCUSS.

Introductive Narrative

Story line intro/

Thoughts have a way of wandering into vivid fantasies or horrible nightmares when one is waiting for important news. I was waiting for important news. Lately, I had been having a few medical problems no one could seem to explain. My doctor had run tests that would show the problems, if any, and the laboratory results were due back today. I sat pensively by the telephone staring at the receiver, then glancing at the clock. When it finally rang, I lunged toward it, but then I paused. Suddenly, I could hear words thundering through my ears and brain telling me I only had a few months to live. My thoughts raced like lightning. If I had but a few short months to live, I would make them the richest ones of my life. . . .

From general to specific

relates to topic question
Simple thesis

First body paragraph developed by description

I would travel first. With only a short time, though, it would most likely be a whirlwind tour of the world. I would want to experience everything: busy streets in Tokyo, cold isolation of the Himalayas, tropical rain of the Amazon, tulips of Holland . . . looking at all the wonders. The people, too, of all different cultures, couldn't be overlooked. Besides seeing all the beauty in the world, I would like to meet the people of the different lands and have conversations. The first weeks of my numbered days would be spent seeing and learning about the world I was leaving.

Appeal to the senses

Descriptive Blend

Use of description in one body paragraph after a blend of alternate approaches in the introduction

Practice Regents' Essay

TOPIC: WHAT JOB, OTHER THAN THE ONE FOR WHICH YOU ARE PREPARING, DO YOU FIND MOST APPEALING?

Attention-getting opening

contrastive

three part thesis

"Yes, Janice and Mark, you and your dating game chaperon will be spending seven sun-filled days and six starry nights at the Hotel La Cucaracha in Cancun, Mexico!" I flip off my television set and start packing my bathing suit and suntan lotion in a suitcase bound for—let me see, where is it this time?—Cancun? No, I am not Janice or Mark, the lucky *Dating Game* couple. I am the notorious *Dating Game* chaperon. I am the insignificant other whose job it is to play Mother over the lovebirds. The job is perfect. I get to travel all over the world, happily watching matched couples fall in love and meeting a few exciting locals at every destination. Who could ask for anything more?

Introduction— combination of description narration, contrast, analysis.

Underline T.V. programs

Answers the question.

First body paragraph developed by description.

Of course, the obvious benefit is the travel. So far, I have visited Italy, Mexico, Hawaii, Switzerland, China, Australia, and every other exotic corner of the earth. I never get bored because one week I find myself bronzing my body on a balmy beach, while the next week I'm whizzing at forty miles per hour down an Alpine ski slope on a ski trip. I sleep in luxurious hotels, dine on gourmet food, and I am paid for it. In addition to these material benefits, the travel is a wonderful history teacher as I learn the background of every place I go. It is a language teacher as I have been able to learn some Spanish, Italian, and French. I see new fashions, watch foreign movies, and experience loads of foreign holidays on each trip.

Appeal to senses—touch, sight, taste, smell, hearing

(After the first body paragraph of description, the author uses alternate approaches for the rest of the essay.)

Regents' Essays Dominated by Description

Entire essay developed primarily by descriptive listing techniques

Actual Regents' Essay Rated 3

TOPIC: WHAT REGION OF THE UNITED STATES DO YOU LIKE THE MOST. WHY?

Appeal to senses

Each region of the country has both good and bad points. The Northeast has many historic sites. The Northwest has the unspoiled beauty of the Pacific mountains. The Midwest has the rich expanses of cultivated land. The southwest has the freedom of its wide open spaces. Despite the attraction of these other regions, the cultural diversity of the Southeast makes it my favorite.

Simple thesis

Listing technique for descriptive, contrastive introduction. Thesis answers question

The many different cultures of the American Southeast provide the visitor and resident with many choices for excitement. There are cities such as Charleston, Savannah, and Williamsburg that portray American's heritage from colonial times. The restaurants and relics of slavery, with its great influx of Blacks from Africa and the Caribbean can be seen in various mini-cultures that thrive throughout the deep South. Also, many names for rivers, lakes and even towns owe their origins to the early Indian tribes such as the Kiowa, Creek, and Cherokee.

Appeal to senses

past influence

Description of cultural diversity.

The Southeast also shows the influence of other nationalities on our societies. Louisiana exhibits the vibrancy of living derived from its French heritage. The architecture is fabulous, the food is delicious, and the sense of romance in the air is intoxicating. Florida owes much of its heritage to the early Spanish settlers there. The pastel stucco houses are a tradition of Florida. Today, Florida still has a large Spanish community. Another subculture is the hill people in the mountains of Tennessee, Kentucky, and North Carolina. These people, often living in poverty, have passed down through the generations many of American's greatest folklore tales. The music and crafts of the mountain inhabitants also provide a glimpse of our past.

transition

Appeal to senses— past influence

transition to further description of cultural diversity

The Southeast is a member of the twentieth century, however. There are thriving business centers such as Miami, Atlanta, and New Orleans, which are also great transportation centers. There are sea and river ports such as Memphis, Mobile, and Roanoke. There are military bases dotting the Southeast from Pope Air Force Base, North Carolina to Camp Shelby, Mississippi.

present

Contrastive transition

listing technique

listing

There are many wonderful things to see and do in the Southeast. The varied geography—from white sandy beaches to peaceful mountain glens, from lazy rolling rivers to spectacular amusement parks—

Listing present attractions

entertains visitors from the world over. But it is the people, the culture, and the rich heritage of the Southeast that make it the most favorable and memorable. Yes, of all the places I have been, the Southeast is the one I favor most.

What will determine your ability to make use of the descriptive approach is once more your awareness of what is going on around you. If you attempt to feel, taste, smell, touch, and see your world, your descriptive powers will be heightened. Take a place as visually dull as your classroom. Jot down sensory details—from the glare of fluorescent lights to the smell of the chalkdust; then you will begin to see the class-room for the first time.

Most of us walk around like zombies in a world waiting to be seen. Even Annie Dillard, naturalist and author, admits that "unless I call my attention to what passes before my eyes, I simply won't see it." Joseph Conrad, who wrote Heart of Darkness and other novels, maintains: "My task . . . is, by the power of the written word, to make you see." E. L. Doctorow, author of Ragtime, adds: "Not that it's raining, but the feel of being rained upon." Focusing on the sensory powers of the descriptive approach will not only make you a better writer on the Regents' essay but make you more alive in the only life you have.

THE ARGUMENTATIVE APPROACH

The mode of development that is required in at least one-fourth of the Regents' topics is the argument. But again the argumentative essay often is complemented by combinations of approaches. When the topic includes the words "attack or defend," the writer needs to take a stand on the issue. Even instructions such as "discuss" and "why" or "why or why not" invite the writers to justify their opinions through logical, persuasive arguments. Once more it is helpful to explain what an argumentative essay is so that the writer of the Regents' essay will be empowered to utilize its strengths:

Definition of the Argumentative Essay

Writing which expresses your opinions and argues in favor of them is argumentative writing. Newspaper editorials and talks of some television and radio commentators are often of this kind. You occasionally use argumentative writing in your class tests when you are asked to give opinions and to support them with facts learned in the course. The purpose of argumentative writing is to convince the reader that the author is right. You must present your arguments clearly if you wish to be convincing.

An argumentative essay must have a statement of opinion supported by paragraphs. This statement commonly known as the thesis is placed at the end of the introductory paragraph. In the formula approach to the argumentative essay, the writers take a stand on one side of the issue and provide three sharp divisions of the thesis to be developed in subsequent body paragraphs. In the "although clause" approach to the topic, the writers place what others say in the introductory adverbial clause of the thesis, and then state two points of their own opinion in the main clause. Because of the time limits on the Regents' test, it is difficult for students to attempt some of the more sophisticated methods of destroying the opposition.

There are several ways to support opinion. Perhaps the most commonly used is the listing of facts or examples (evidence) in support of your stand. You may also prove your point by giving reasonable arguments arrived at through logical thinking. A combination of evidence and reasonable arguments is the most effective way to develop the essay. At the end of the essay, you should add a <u>summarizing paragraph</u> to clinch your point.

The order of ideas in an argumentative paragraph

The ideas in the argumentative essay move from lesser to greater importance—saving the most powerful arguments and the most convincing evidence until the last body paragraph.

Outline of "Although Clause" Structure

(four sentences)

Introduction—Three sentences and then "although clause" thesis. Place your stand in the main clause as follows:

Although many people are against _____ ,
   (some)
I favor it because of _____ and _____ . (your stand)
                              OR
Although many people favor _____ , I am against it
   (some)
because of _____ and _____ . (your stand)

First body paragraph—(Contrastive—What others say—use listing:

(four sentences)

   1. Some say _____

   2. Others maintain _____

   3. Still others argue _____

   4. Transition below.

<u>Important transitional statement to your point of view:</u>
But the positive/negative effects of _____ far outweigh the negative/positive arguments.

Second body paragraph—your point developed. (150 words)

(5–7 sentences)

3rd body paragraph—Your most powerful point developed. (150 words)

(5–7 sentences)

Conclusion/summary.

(four sentences)

The "although clause" has become a favorite among my RTP students because often they have difficulty in finding three sharp divisions of an argumentative topic. Instead, upon selecting a Regents' topic, they jot down arguments for and against. After determining their stand, they choose two sharply divided points to develop. Then they gather together the opposition's arguments for a contrasting paragraph. Listing what others say for one paragraph allows them to concentrate on their two strongest points for the remaining two body paragraphs. Because these alternate approaches should free the writers to develop their topics in a variety of ways, the Regents' essays that follow not only show close adherence to the suggested diagram of the "although clause" but also reveal other helpful patterns.

Regents' Essay Developed by the "Although Clause" Approach

The following student essay illustrates not only the "although clause" approach but also the use of suggested transitions to push away the point of view of others and to persuade the audience to adopt her stand on the issue:

TOPIC: WOULD YOU BE BETTER OFF IF YOU DIDN'T OWN A TELEVISION SET? DISCUSS.

Attention-getting opening

What others say

Over seventy-five percent of American households own a television set. It is said that we Americans watch an average of six and a half hours of television each day. "While the world watches America, America watches television" is a quote I often chuckle about. Television has become a very powerful force in shaping public opinion. Although many people feel that TV has some beneficial qualities, I think that the medium has hampered my personal growth by promoting passive involvement and by conveying stereotypes.

Verifiable statistics

Although clause—Author's two points

Students memorize transitions to quickly develop contrastive paragraph.

Some people say that television is useful because it can enlighten and inform us. Others maintain that the news broadcasts and documentaries allow us to bring the world into our homes. Still others argue that science and all its marvels can be appreciated in the comfort of our living rooms or that millions of children have gained essential knowledge from *Sesame Street.* But I personally feel that the negative effects of the medium have outweighed any positive aspects of television.

Use of transitions connecting what others say

Important transitional expression

Topic sentence from general to specific

Television, by its very nature, promotes passive involvement. Very few programs actually challenge the viewer. It seems that television was created to entertain. In the 1950's, families watched comedy shows or situation comedy shows as a means of recreation. Television acts as a one-way communication system towards its audience. For this reason, television rarely promotes real learning. A study just released emphasized the fact that TV actually promotes aggression and dulls the senses. In fact, I can't name the last really stimulating show I saw.

What author says

Topic sentence

specific listing of programs

Another problem with most television shows is the stereotypes they convey. Shouldn't my life have turned out better? I mean, *The Brady Bunch* brainwashed me regarding families. There was no problem that could not be solved; life always had happy endings. The show *Room 222* portrayed how high school was going to be; how different the actual experience was! Most female characters in the 1960's and 1970's were depicted either as bird brains or evil, nasty people not to be taken seriously as they plotted to destroy others and were foiled in their attempts. Even the popular shows, *I Love Lucy* and later *Here's Lucy* failed to portray Lucy as being re-

What author says

Effects of stereotypes

Underline TV programs shown in italics.

spected or capable but mainly as a comic conniver. Today the stereotypes continue regardless of the feeble attempts to upgrade the quality.

Student answers question

Even though some say the "boob tube" has its merits, I believe I would be better off if I didn't own a television set. It seems TV simply does more damage rather than create positive results. It's incredible to think of the number of hours I've literally wasted sitting in front of primetime nonsense. I want to read more books, have more friends, and be more productive. Moreover, our communities need more involvement from citizens that could reduce their viewing to a mere ten hours per week rather than the weekly average of forty hours per person.

Summary

Author's opinion

Personal list

Application to others

The next essay on growing old in American makes use of the "although clause" but develops one point in depth, rather than the listing technique utilized in the contrastive second paragraph of the previous composition on television.

Practice Regents' Essay

TOPIC: WHY ARE SO MANY PEOPLE AFRAID OF GROWING OLD?

Reference to familiar song at beginning and end

America is a society obsessed with youth. The phrase "America the Beautiful" refers to more than just its land; it reflects the emphasis that Americans have placed on physical beauty. Aging is inevitable in every society, but in the United States it has become a burden. Although conditions are improving for the elderly, growing old in America is depressing because of economic conditions and vulnerability to crime.

Analysis of cultural values

Contrastive clause—author's two points

One point fully developed

The bulk of America's population is comprised of the so-called "baby boomers." Usually well educated and extremely career oriented, they are changing the meaning of growing old. Often referred to as "yuppies," this group has become obsessed with longevity. They are eating healthier and have incorporated exercise into their daily routine. In addition, they are planning for their futures by investing in such creative plans as IRA's, stocks, bonds, and Keogh accounts. However, not everyone can afford these luxuries.

Development of contrastive clause

transition

Important transition

Topic sentence

For America's senior citizens things today are not as bright as they may be for those fortunate citizens who prepare for the future. Twelve percent of American's population is over sixty-five. However, their income is roughly fifty percent less than that of the average American household. Usually dependent upon fixed incomes, they face enormous hardships. These aged have no defense against the rising cost of food, housing, utilities, and the staggering increases in health care. As they become less mobile, they are confined to a specific area that must fulfill their every need. This isolation in turn eliminates their options to improve their economic situation.

In addition, the elderly are often prey to criminals. Having lost much of their agility, they have become a target for street crimes. These older Americans often keep many of their personal possessions either on their person or in their homes, creating a scenario ideal for purse snatchers and burglars. Hoping to better themselves financially, they are prime candidates for investment scams and felonious investments. Cognizant of their mortality and fearing death, they are victimized by religious charlatans who promise them health and salvation in exchange for money.

Conditions are improving for Americans as we begin to grow old together. As we become more aware of the suffering of our aged, we are making provisions to prevent this deprivation from happening to us. However, at present, our elderly are locked to fixed incomes, fixed locations, and society's attitudes. For the senior citizen "America the Beautiful" is an expression full of empty promises.

One final word about the merits of the "although clause" is in order–not only because it enables writers to quickly organize and emphasize their strongest points but also because it appeals to the audience who reads the essays. During the RTP Seminar, I point out that the raters' instruction booklet on page 24 praises the approach calling it "meritorious" and "sophisticated." Moreover the greatest emphasis in education today is on critical thinking, and this technique illustrates the willingness to look at both sides of the issue.

Clustering of Controversial Issues

Analyzing the list of the 493 Regents' topics, I found some natural clustering of controversial issues that allows for group discussion and debate. RTP classes may find that one class hour can be devoted to discussing the pros and cons of one or more categories. Similar class periods may be used to address all the clusterings. Or the students preparing for the Regents' test may obtain some comfort from seeing the topics listed and from receiving clarification of terms. Others may gain confidence from realizing that they have a working knowledge of the majority of the issues. Certainly students are more eager to read the newspaper or discuss editorials in the USA Today if they know they are preparing for passing specific Regents' essay questions. By reading about both sides of the issue in the debate page of USA Today, they are also gathering ideas for the development of the "although clause." But the greatest benefit of addressing the clustering of argumentative topics is the student's realization that he/she has become aware of the socio-politico-economic issues of our society and can more easily and confidently communicate at home, at school, or on the job.

Exercises for Clusters of Argumentative Topics

A. Select one clustering.
B. Discuss in small groups.
C. Identify pros and cons.
D. Be tolerant of others' points of view.
E. Other exercises to be applied to any or all clusters are as follows:
    1. Identify terms.
    2. Test your understanding of issue.
    3. Brainstorm to find major arguments for or against.
    4. Determine your stand.
    5. Compose a thesis.
       a. Use formula thesis.
         or
       b. Use although clause.
    6. Compose three sentences leading to thesis. (introduction)
F. Add on to your knowledge and skills by reading, listening, and informally discussing issues.
    1. Scan newspapers for references to issues.
    2. Read argumentative essays in The Polishing Cloth.
    3. Read debate page of USA Today.
    4. Listen to radio and television with topics in mind.
    5. Discuss issues with family and friends.

The Clusters

   1. <u>Political Issues</u>

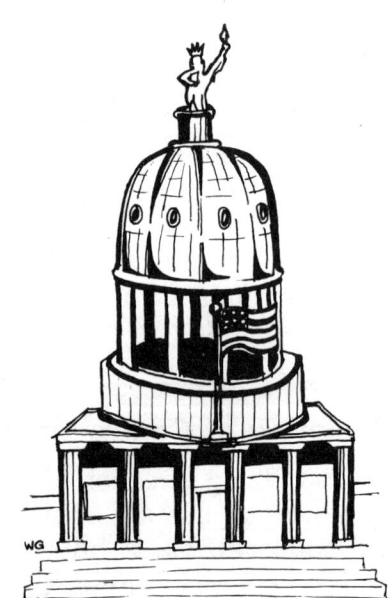

      Mandatory Voting
      Government Regulation of Child Care
      Policy on Homeless
      Limiting Terms of Congressmen/Presidents
      Funding Space Program
      A Woman President
      Early Results (effect on voter)
      Nuclear Freeze
      Deficit Spending
      Social Programs versus Military Spending
      Pari-mutual Betting—Legalized Gambling
      Sales Tax on Necessities
      Work Programs for Welfare Recipients
      Private Sector versus Public Funding of Projects
      Cutting Social Security Payments to Elderly
      Retaining the 55 mph Speed Limit

2. Education Issues

Technical Training versus Liberal Arts
Dwindling Financial Aid
Overemphasis on the Computer
Extended School Year
Searches and Seizures
Prayer in the Schools
Tax Credits for Private School
Emphasis on Grades
Sex Education
Corporal Punishment
Mainstreaming the Handicapped
Student Activities Fees
Funding with Property Tax
AIDS in the Classroom
CPR in the Curriculum
Back to Basics—Watered-down Curriculum
Effect of Extracurricular Activities
Plagiarism/Cheating Policies
Requirement of Second Language
Physical Education Requirement
Competency Tests for Teachers
Required College Courses in Public Speaking
Publishing of College Faculty Evaluations

3. Topics Related to Crime

Capital Punishment
Mandatory Sentencing
Rights of Victim
Rehabilitation
Prison Reform
Plea Bargaining
Gun Control
Media Coverage
Control of Terrorism
Mental Illness Issue
Regulation of Drug Traffic
Education of Prisoners
Reluctance to Report Crime
Citizen's Right to Defend
Increase in Prison Construction
Respect for Police Officers

4. Foreign Policy Issues

Our Role as Peace-keeper
Sharing Food Supplies
Dropping Aid to Nations (Those Against Our Policies)
Negotiation with Russia
Restricting Political Refugees
Selling Arms
Nuclear Proliferation

Human Rights
Restricting Foreign Car Imports
Future of United Nations

5. Legal Issues

Open Adoption
Marriage Contracts
Living Wills
Polygraph Tests in Court/Workplace
Single Parent Adoption
Right to Privacy
Raising the Drinking Age
Legalization of Marijuana
Televised Court Proceedings
Restrictions on Owners of Pit Bulldogs
Requiring Safety Belts
Reinstatement of Draft
Father's Right to Custody
Book Banning
Right to Die
Banning Non-returnable Drink Containers
Banning of Billboards
Abolishing Happy Hours
Abolishing Tipping

6. Environmental Issues

Use of Public Land
Chemical Dumps
Nuclear Power
Greenhouse Effect
Air Pollution
Smoker versus Non-Smoker
Offshore Drilling
Auto Emission Regulation
Funding Public Transportation
Nuclear Waste Disposal
Destruction of Rain Forests
Conservation of Natural Resources

7. Women's Issues

Popularity of Beauty Contests
Combat Duty for Women
Welfare "Pink Poverty" (Women as Single Heads
    of Households)
Women as Managers
Women in the Work Force
Division of Duties in the Home
Women's Liberation
Birth Control—Notification of Parents of Minors

8. Health

   Physicians'/Dentists' Advertising
   The Rising Cost of Health Care
   Organ Donations
   Stress in our Society
   Testing for AIDS
   Crash Diets
   Obsession with Physical Fitness
   Benefits or Consequences of Running
   Animal Organ Transplants in Humans
   Government Health Care Plan
   Passive Smoking
   Overemphasis on Youth/Plastic Surgery
   Ban on Advertising Alcohol/Cigarettes
   Furnishing Drugs to Addicts
   Noise Pollution Regulation

9. Sports

   Organized Sports for Children
   Violence in Sports
   Education of College Athlete
   High-priced Athlete
   Recruitment Policies
   Banning Boxing
   Subsidization of Olympic Teams
   Emphasis on Winning
   Funding of High School Sports Programs
   Use of Olympics for Propaganda
   Drugs and the Professional Athlete

The Expository Approach

One freshman writer remarked that when I introduced the <u>expository essay</u>, all she could think of was a garbage can. I told her I would have preferred that she visualize a more savory image such as multi-flavored neapolitan ice cream or even the one dish casserole. But she countered with the remark that since the expository essay contained so many types of development, no other reference was quite so apt. You can be the judge as you analyze the following definition:

Definition of the Expository Essay

An expository theme is the most common theme style used in developing the Regents' topics. Exposition can contain definitions, comparison and contrast, examples, facts, incidents, and arguments. It often combines several techniques used in types of themes that you have already written in composition classes. In all expository essays, you will carefully construct a thesis sentence in the first paragraph or introduction and will support it with paragraphs. The thesis will predict and control your essay development.

An expository essay can be compared with a discussion. Just as the class will have panel discussions and will explore all aspects of a topic, so you shall be composing a thesis statement and developing it thoroughly. An argumentative theme can be compared with a debate. Just as debaters must take a stand and must attempt to convince the audience to their way of thinking, so writers of an argumentative essay must adopt a definite side and write to persuade their readers. Therefore, the difference between an expository and an argumentative essay is that an expository theme does not necessarily contain a definite stand; the writer analyzes the entire issue. Sometimes the writers present their ideas and let the reader decide, but in writing a passing Regents' essay, the writers are expected to come to a careful conclusion after considering various aspects of the topic. Thus, writers of expository themes do not write with the purpose of convincing the readers but with the idea of informing them.

Transitions used in an expository essay are as follows: and, or/nor, also, moreover, furthermore, indeed, in fact, first, second, for instance, for example, for one thing, similarly, likewise, therefore, thus, so, and so, hence, consequently, finally, on the whole, all in all, in other words, in short, frequently, occasionally, in particular, in general, specifically, especially, usually, of course, no doubt, doubtless, to be sure, granted (that), certainly, but, however, yet, on the contrary, not at all, surely, no, still, nevertheless, not withstanding, although, though, whereas, because, since, for, if provided, in case, unless, lest, when, as if, as though, even if.

The knowledge that the major clusterings of all the 493 published Regents' topics reflect the discussion of expository approach to essay writing suggests that one way of preparing for the Regents' test is to have small group discussions. If you discuss with your classmates the major clusters of the Regents' topics listed below, you will have a good chance of actually writing on one of these issues during the testing period. The topics often overlap as the numbers beside them suggest:

Discussion Topics Based on the Major Clusters

These discussion topics reflect the major clustering of the 493 Regents' topics:

1. What's Happening to the American Family? (55–60 topics)

2. The Quality of Television (50–55 topics)

3. Public School Education in the United States—Strengths or Weaknesses (65–70 topics)

4. The Economic State of the Nation (25–30 topics)

5. Growing Old in America (45–50 topics)

6. Crime—Cause or Prevention (55–60 topics)

7. America's Role in the Free World (25–30 topics)

8. The Defense of the United States (15–20 topics)

9. Health and Physical Fitness (40–45 topics)

10. The State of the Environment (10–15 topics)

Plan for Discussion of Major Clustering of Topics

1. Gather in discussion groups of no more than five.

2. Choose one topic—one clustering.

3. Jot down any ideas about the topic that come to mind.

4. Talk over your thoughts with your classmates as you write.

   a. You will learn from each other as ideas are introduced.

   b. One idea will bring out another.

   c. Consult pages 9–10 for some verifiable statistics.

5. Look for key words to reflect ideas or to tie them together.

6. Choose three <u>sharp</u> divisions of the topic you could write five—seven sentences about.

   a. You may have to combine points.

   b. You should choose your own division to reflect your strength.

   c. Your decision may be the same or different from other members in the group.

7. Test each division chosen by jotting down ideas under it.

8. Compose thesis.

9. Read it to the group to test for clarity and flow.

10. You and your group members have just prepared your minds for 50–55 topics on the Regents' essay exam.

Optional: Plan for Formal Discussion, Composition, and Checklist. (See pages 12–13)

11. Your instructor may ask group members to discuss their ideas in front of the class. (Particularly if each group was discussing a different clustering.) Your instructor may refer you to the rules for panel discussion and the evaluation blank on pages 14–15.

    Your instructor may ask you to write an essay about this topic in a simulated Regents' booklet. It might be a timed or untimed essay. **Bring a dictionary to class.**

13. After you have written your essay, complete the checklist on page 29 of the Regents' Test Preparation Seminar section of this book.

14. Assess where you have zeros on the checklist and work to improve those areas. You are in control.

Application of Plan

Let's apply this plan to one of the clusterings—the first—"What's Happening to the American Family?" As you <u>jot down ideas</u> and <u>discuss</u> them, you may have listed the high divorce rate (50%), one parent families, mobility or transiency, lack of communication, smaller size, working mothers, latchkey children, drug problems, emphasis on "meism," women's liberation, influence of television. After such a listing of ideas, <u>key words</u> may come to mind such as <u>"fragmentation"</u> or <u>"change."</u> Now select three sharp divisions of the topic. Choose those divisions because you feel strongly about them, and that high level of interest will enable you to add more details. You might have to combine several ideas to create a division. Test each division you choose to see if you have enough to say. For example, after the group brainstorming of the topic "What's Happening to the American Family?", student Maggie McElreath chose as her sharp divisions increasing mobility, women's liberation, and the negative influence of television. Her jot list to test her knowledge of those divisions was as follows:

Mobility

smaller size
career development
transfer
economic changes
change over to industry from agriculture
leaving relatives
leaving friends
losing roots

Women's Liberation

working women
changing roles
delegation of former roles
lack of communication
frequency of divorce
latchkey children
drug problems

Negative influence of television

emphasis on individual
"meism"
portrayal of non-traditional families
put down of Father Knows Best; Leave It to Beaver; Happy Days

Maggie was then satisfied that she had enough to write about in each area and elected to follow all of the 14 steps listed on pages 86–87 to enhance the possibility of passing the Regents' exam. In the process, she became fully aware of the major issues facing our nation and the world as a whole. She read the newspaper, listened to the radio, and watched television to help gather ideas and add verifiable statistics. Engaging in discussion with her classmates, forming and refining her ideas, and then writing on them allowed her to connect her writing with the real world. For the first time, she could confidently integrate and synthesize ideas and exercise conceptual thinking. The essay that follows is a result of that in-depth process of preparation.

Essay Resulting from the Application of the Plan

WHAT'S HAPPENING TO THE AMERICAN FAMILY?

Key words

The American family has traditionally been a bastion of stability by having well-defined roots and well-defined roles for each member. The American family, however, has inadvertently become the target of many fragmenting forces. We are now seeing significant changes in some of its long established traditions. The most evident and far reaching changes have taken place because of increasing mobility, women's liberation, and the negative influence television has had on the family image.

Three sharp divisions

To begin with, the family that remains with a well rooted community for any length of time is almost unheard of in 1990's. The change over in our society from one based on agriculture to one based on industry has helped promote mobility in America—giving rise to a new transient family. This trend, while being a positive force in career development, has had negative effects on the family as a whole. Easier mobility has allowed families to transfer from one location to another while leaving behind many of the segments that have traditionally helped shape and hold the family unit together: aunts, uncles, grandparents, long-term friendships, and community groups. While mobility may have broadened Americans' horizons, it has also chipped away at their foundations.

Meanwhile, women encouraged by the Women's Liberation Movement have moved from the traditional role of wife and mother to a broader range of new professions and priorities. This trend has caused many changes to occur within the family unit. Women have traditionally been the caretakers of the family, watching over the young, ailing, and old. However, with so many women now employed in the work force, we are seeing the care of the family members delegated to agencies outside of the family. The women's movement, while productive on an individual basis, has inadvertently taken some of the cohesiveness out of the family unit.

Finally, television's obsession with the individual has diverted our attention and admiration away from the family and family members. The result has been a subliminal devaluation of the family. The "me-generation" of the seventies has continued its exploration of self, as reflected in television advertising and programming. Traditional family roles are under siege by the disrupting television stereotypes that aren't supportive of the family. We are continually being bombarded by television's portrayal of the wonderful aspects of developing our own individualism versus what it obviously considers the uninspiring development of the family through interdependence—a necessary step in the realization of a well-working, traditional family.

While the American family is still an important unit within our society, it has suffered considerably under the stress placed on it by our changing social structure. Over the past fifty years, the American family has been assaulted from a variety of angles.

Progress has marched on, and sometimes the <u>unit under its bloody heel</u> has been the American family. One wonders how a structure, even one as basic as the family unit, can long endure under such pressure.

ADVANTAGES OF ALTERNATE APPROACHES

What should these <u>definitions</u> and <u>discussion</u> of the <u>four basic approaches to composition</u>—the narrative, descriptive, argumentative, and expository—<u>do for you as a writer</u> preparing for the Regents' essay test?

1. They should place you in control of your ideas and empower you to develop the Regents' topics in the most meaningful, effective manner.

2. They should allow you to see the richness and variety of ways to communicate and free you to make use of your strengths as a writer.

3. They should help you focus on the key to passing the Regents' essay—knowing yourself well and <u>valuing your own experiences</u>, <u>ideas</u>, <u>opinions</u>.

4. They may make you realize that although the RTP course is an intensive preparation to pass the Regents' essay, through focusing on issues you are also connecting the composition classroom with the outside world and becoming a more informed, aware member of society.

PRACTICE WITH PAIRED TOPICS

When preparing to pass the Regent's essay test, you will find that there is no substitute for writing full-length, timed essays. When polling RTP instructors statewide as to their best advice to their students, I heard again and again—"Write; write; write." The more you write the more comfortable you will feel when adjusting your writing style and content to answer the topic assigned. In fact, one of my students remarked, "I have written so many essays that I now feel that I could write on anything." Listed below are the pairings of the Regents' topics as they appeared on test booklets in past quarters. In fact, these paired topics are often repeated quarterly. Note that in most cases one topic within the student's life experience is combined with one outside, requiring knowledge of history, literature, or socio-economic-political issues. Your instructor may want you to spend class time discussing the topics with a classmate, choosing one, and writing a thesis jointly or separately. Although various exercises can be applied to these pairings, the following steps will be very helpful in assuring a passing grade on the Regents' essay test.

90

1. Read both topics carefully.

2. Underline key words that help you understand the question or statement.

3. Choose the topic closest to you—the one to which you can add the most details and examples.

4. Visualize yourself in the topic chosen.

5. Jot down any ideas that come to mind—brainstorm.

6. Group ideas; select sharp divisions; avoid repetition

7. Compose a thesis using the approach that is not only most successful for you but also fits the topic.

8. Write an essay in one hour.

9. Remember to leave time for proofing. Check for your major errors.

10. Use a dictionary for the last fifteen minutes, if needed.

Paired Essay Topics on Actual Regents' Test

- Do you prefer shopping at a large shopping center or at downtown stores? Discuss.

- Why is college football so popular? Discuss.

- What do you consider to be your duties as an American citizen? Discuss.

- Archaeologists have learned much about the lives of first-century Romans from the excavations of houses buried by lava at Pompeii. Suppose that your home were preserved just as it is now. What conclusions about life in the 1980's might this evidence lead future archaeologists to draw?

- If you could change one thing about your childhood, what would it be? Discuss.

- Presidential greatness is often debated by professional historians. Which U.S. president would you identify as the greatest? Justify your selection.

- Many states have enacted laws banning all non-returnable drink containers. Should Georgia pass such a law? Why or why not?

- What types of movies do you prefer? Explain.

- Would you prefer to rear a family in the city or the country? Explain why.

- Should the media show more respect for celebrities' desire for privacy? Discuss.

- Are elementary and high schools adequately meeting the needs of their students? Discuss.

- If you could make one scientific discovery in your lifetime, what would it be? Why?

- Should parents encourage their teenage children to work even if the family does not need the money?

- Is it better to have brothers and sisters than to be an only child? Explain.

- If you had the power to change any event in history (outcome of an election, who won a war, etc.), which would you choose to change, and why?

- Is it beneficial for a high school graduate to work full-time for a year before entering college? Why or why not?

- Apart from chronological age, what are some major differences between an adolescent and an adult? Explain.

- If you were among the first colonizers of a new planet in the twenty-first century, what would you want your fellow colonists to transport from the planet Earth? Explain.

- How can parents promote good reading habits in their children? Discuss.

- Should the government allow unlimited numbers of refugees from political oppression to enter the U.S.? Discuss.

- Do you long for the past or look eagerly toward the future? Explain.

- Should court proceedings be televised? Explain why or why not.

- Should women in the military services be assigned combat duties? Discuss.

- What makes one college course more enjoyable than another? Explain.

- We now have more people over 65 than at any other time. What are the major effects of this increased proportion of older people? Discuss.

- Should colleges make it optional for students to pay activity fees? Discuss why or why not.

- Is there any job that you would absolutely refuse to take? Explain.

- It has been said that "Evil, like good, has its own heroes." Name some characters that you consider to be "evil heroes." Explain.

- Explain the chief reasons why students drop out of school.

- Should the United States offer foreign aid only to those nations which support our policies? Discuss.

- Should children be disciplined by physical punishment? Discuss.

- Discuss some of the pressures of college students.

- How does your public image differ from your private self?

- Should the government increase taxes to help improve the standard of living of poor people? Discuss why or why not.

- How do you account for the popularity of horror films? Discuss.

- Discuss the importance that a relative (other than a parent) has had in your life.

- Is noise pollution becoming a serious threat to the welfare of Americans? Discuss.

- What was the most important event of your life? Discuss why this event was so important.

- Why do so many people like to have collections of something (antiques, coins, stamps, dolls)? Discuss.

- Which do you believe has been most influential in your life—good luck (chance) or good decisions? Explain.

- What, in your opinion, are some of the reasons so many people have pets? Discuss.

- The United States has never had a female president. To what do you attribute this? Discuss.

- Should college students be required to take physical education courses? Why or why not?

- How do you think our future will be influenced by the great influx of foreign products into the United States? Explain.

- Should the custom of tipping be abolished? Explain why or why not.

- If you were to set up a personal museum of the most significant objects you own, what would you include and why?

- Most people consider themselves part of a particular generation. Discuss what you consider the most important values of your generation.

- What kind of information would you want to obtain before making a major purchase such as a car or stereo system?

- If you had the power to do one thing to improve the world, what would you do? Discuss.

- Several communities have recently passed laws making it illegal for bars to promote the consumption of alcohol through sales specials such as happy hours, two-for-one hours, and ladies' night. Do you agree or disagree that these laws are needed? Discuss.

- If you could choose any culture or society, which one would you choose to live in? Discuss.

- Explain why you do or do not vote.

- What characteristics do you regard as important in a person you would choose as a friend?

- Why have the Southern states been gaining population in the last two decades? Discuss.

- Should an introduction to art, music, and drama be a part of every college student's education? Explain why or why not.

- Should fathers be given the same chance as mothers to gain custody of their minor children? Discuss.

- Explain the chief reasons why students drop out of high school.

- Many families today are growing home vegetable gardens. Discuss some reasons for this.

- Discuss ways to increase the public's respect for elected officials.

- What career, other than the one for which you are preparing, do you find most appealing? Explain.

- What do you hope to accomplish within the next ten years? Explain.

- Should the government increase taxes to help improve the standard of living of poor people? Discuss why or why not.

- The evidence shows that for many reasons the family-owned and family-run small farm is a vanishing American institution. Should this situation cause concern in American society? Why or why not.

- Of the sources of entertainment which are popular today, which do you find least appealing? Discuss.

- If you were to be deprived of one of your five senses (sight, touch, small, taste, and hearing) which one would you most hate to give up? Explain.

- Should the school year be extended to include longer hours and more days required to obtain a high school diploma? Discuss.

- Every applicant for a Georgia's driver's license must choose whether to be an organ donor. Would you choose to be a donor? Explain why or why not.

- The Supreme Court has recently ruled that public schools have the right to conduct searches of students' persons and property when there is reasonable cause to suspect the presence of weapons or drugs. Do you support or oppose such searches? Explain.

- Is it better for a political leader to be feared instead of loved? Why or why not?

- What is the best advice you ever got? Explain.

FINAL APPROACHES

Saving Your Essays

When you have finished your RTP course or any other composition class, it is very important that you save your essays. They are a record of how you handle timed and untimed essay writing. As you review them before the Regents' test, you will be heartened by your improvement in the five week period, will be reminded what worked and did not work for you, and will be able to focus on the major errors you will want to avoid. Perhaps the most important reason for saving your essays is that they contain your thoughts at one point in time—personal opinions on issues of the day and reflections on your life. You will become aware that once you are accustomed

THROUGH WORDS, A PERSON CAN
SHARE AN EXCITING EXPERIENCE.

to the routine of frequent essay writing, some fresh, inspired thinking will emerge under the pressure of the timed essay.

Preparing for the Test Date

Physical Preparation

As the date for the Regents' test approaches, make sure that you have all the equipment to pass the test—two erasable blue or black pens—two number two pencils—a dictionary or speller you have used often, and your own wrist watch. Wear layered clothing to adjust to the temperature of the room, and visit the test site ahead of time. If possible, sit down and write an essay in the test place; at least get the feel of the desks provided.

Find out what time of day you are most alert and sign-up for that test period. Be sure to get the appropriate amount of sleep and nourishment so that you feel physically strong for the two hour exam. Be sure to arrive early on the day of the test but not so early that you will be forced to sit for long periods of time. Some students like to walk around the building to work off nervous energy. And recognize that the energy can work for you when you take the test.

Mental Preparation

To avoid feeling tense during the exam, practice relaxation techniques during your RTP practice tests or other exams. Whether they are deep-breathing exercises, focusing on relaxing each part of your body from the toes to the scalp on your head, or closing your eyes and visualizing your favorite vacation spot—one or more of these techniques will work for you. Taking the test with an RTP classmate or classmates who have been supportive of you during the course will also relax you. You will feel

Feel the dream power!

more comfortable if you see them in the room or better yet if they are writing beside you.

Finally, weeks before the exam, you should visualize yourself passing the exam. Picture yourself getting a topic on which you can write easily, developing that topic, even feeling some creative flow, and walking out of the test site with a feeling of satisfaction—maybe elation. Certainly visualization needs to have some substance behind it, but you have put forth the effort. You are better prepared than the majority of Regents' test takers. You have alternate approaches to handle the topics; you have found which ones work best for you. You have worked hard on writing essays, correcting your errors, and proofing your papers. You deserve to pass, and visualizing it will help make that passing become a reality.

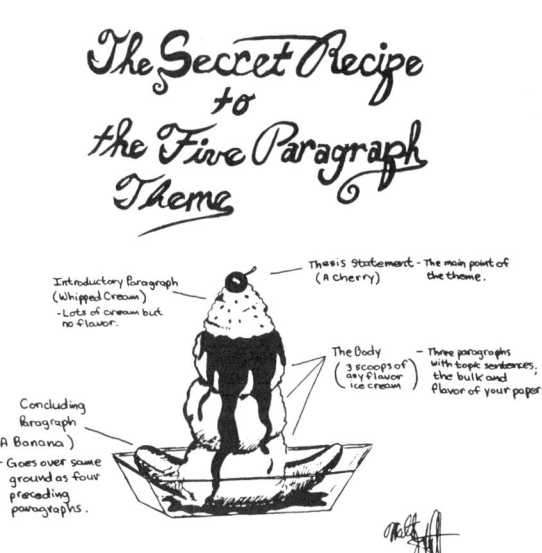

The Secret Recipe to the Five Paragraph Theme

Introductory Paragraph (Whipped Cream) - Lots of cream but no flavor.

Thesis Statement - The main point of (A cherry) the theme.

The Body (3 scoops of any flavor ice cream) - Three paragraphs with topic sentences, the bulk and flavor of your paper.

Concluding Paragraph (A Banana) - Goes over same ground as four preceding paragraphs.

Entertain the reader with your ideas—
not your misplaced modifiers.

The obese woman was arguing with a polite fireman in a blue dress carrying a white purse.

Mark was stung by a wasp picking daffodils in his garden.

Twelve long stemmed roses were brought by a delivery man in a pink box.

There was a woman standing on one foot while the other is resting on its heel reading a People magazine.

RTP—A Personalized Approach to Grammar

More than any composition course offered in the University System of Georgia, the Regents' Test Preparation is personalized. Your strengths and weaknesses in writing are the substance of the course. It is all about you and your relationship to the world around you as revealed in the many essays you will write. The intensive nature of the five plus weeks of preparation should allow you—perhaps for the first time—to analyze your writing skills and to know what works for you.

An integral component of passing the Regents' essay is your knowledge of your most serious errors—not your classmates' grammar problems—yours. Therefore grammar will not be studied in isolation. The only grammar errors you will focus on are those you commit. Your RTP instructor will help you by marking your errors with correction symbols such as the ones included on page 102. In addition your classmates will aid you in spotting your errors as you exchange essays with them. You will find your fellow students most supportive as you prepare together for the big game. They may give you helpful hints as to what has worked for them. Seek out and accept all the assistance you can get until some idea clicks—some way of looking at your grammar errors works for you.

Note that the definition of errors on page 102 lists the most serious first. The CS/frag/RO and sv/agr errors will be the most distracting to the raters and are listed as three star errors on the RTP Seminar Checklist on page 27. You will want to try to avoid the big four and to proof for them in the final ten to fifteen minutes of the testing period. Use an erasable pen to mark words and punctuation you are unsure of. Then erase the marks so that you will not draw the raters' attention.

WRITING AND PROOFING YOUR ESSAY

A most valuable skill that you need to learn when preparing to pass the Regents' essay test is that of proofreading. Then you can become your own editor. Learning to proof effectively will make you feel as if you are in control of your own writing. Remember that your instructor will not be sitting beside you. You must learn to spot those problems that show up often in your compositions.

But most importantly you should avoid letting your concern with spelling and grammar errors interrupt your creative flow of ideas. The limit on the use of a dictionary or a speller until the last fifteen minutes actually helps you concentrate on content and unity of ideas. The following are some hints that help you proof while at the same time remind you of the importance of the clarity of the whole composition.

1. Write while your ideas are hot. Your writing will flow naturally, and you will avoid choppy, stringy sentences.

2. Then let your essay cool. Close your eyes for a few minutes after writing your Regents' test. When you proof, you will see your own writing more objectively; you will more readily spot your errors.

3. Use all of the time remaining in the test period by proofing your paper as many times as possible. Budget at least ten minutes, more if you can.

    a. First quickly check the whole. Is the thesis clear? Do the paragraphs support it? Check to see if the words used in the Regents' topic question you have chosen are accurately spelled. Misspelling words provided for you is a major mark against you.

b. Then proofread by reading <u>each sentence</u> from left to right and from bottom to top on the page; in other words, <u>read backwards</u> so that you can catch spelling errors. Remember to erase any pen marks alerting raters. *Using a speller may be more helpful in quickly checking your errors than struggling with a cumbersome dictionary. Look especially for major errors that you know you often make.

c. If time permits, proofread by whispering. You should practice this art so that it will not bother those around you. Pay special attention to the sound of words, particularly check for endings.

Although these are steps in proofing that help others, find out what works for you by using up all your time in each practice session in your RTP class. Since proofing is an art, it must be practiced when writing every essay—not just those written in the last week before the test date.

comma splice *(CS)*	two complete thoughts separated by a comma
fragment *(frag)*	an incomplete thought
run-on *(RO)*	two complete thoughts without any mark of punctuation between them
subject-verb agreement *(SV agr)*	the lack of agreement in number between subject and verb sv agr Example: We <u>was</u> present.
pronoun-antecedent agreement *(P A agr)*	the lack of agreement in number between the pronoun and the word it refers to—the antecedent P A agr Example: Everyone seeing the sight must feel <u>their</u> heart leap.
Sp	misspelling
dangling modifier *(DM)*	a dangling phrase containing a verbal—that is, a participle, an infinitive, or a gerund—having no word it can modify DM Example: To see <u>better,</u> my desk was changed.
misplaced modifier *(MM)*	a word or a group of words modifying the wrong word MM Example: <u>Hanging on the wall,</u> we saw a new picture.
reference *(ref)*	broad or implied or confusing reference to persons, places, or things Example: One should always salute the flag of the United States. *ref* <u>This</u> is a sign of loyalty.
diction *(d/)*	incorrect choice of word
K/	awkwardness in sentence construction
Coh/	coherence—lack of clarity—not clear to the reader
llism	parallelism—lack of balance on both sides of the coordinating conjunction llism Example: I enjoy swimming, hiking, and to fish.
cst/	choppy or stringy sentences

p/	punctuation—Commas must be placed after:
	1. introductory adverb clauses
	2. introductory verbal phrases
	3. introductory prepositional phrases (if more than three words or to prevent misreading)
	4. commas before co-ordinating conjunctions containing two complete sentences
	5. commas in a series
	6. commas setting off: appositives
	                              nouns of address
	                              parenthetical expressions

¶ = paragraphing

shift - changing voice, person, or tense within a sentence or paragraph

lc - lower case   poss = possessive case

SPELLING

English spelling offers many complicated problems, but improvement in conquering your spelling errors is a matter of determination. It is simply not true that there are many people who "just can't spell." There are a few who have visual or neural difficulties that require medical or psychological attention. If your poor spelling should result from one of these serious deficiencies, you will want to contact the center for special academic support or counseling center for assessment of your problem.

In some cases the difficulty in spelling arises from the way you were taught to read. If you were taught to read by recognizing whole words at once (sight-reading), instead of by syllables—if in first grade you saw and recognized cat instead of c-a-t, and later separate instead of sep-a-rate—you may never really have seen the words you misspell. <u>It is not always your fault that you are a poor speller, but it will be if you remain one</u>. Most poor spellers have never taken the trouble to learn to spell conventionally, usually because they have seen no need for learning if spell-check or dictionaries are readily available. But the Regents' essay test demands that you focus on your spelling problems because you have only fifteen minutes with the dictionary or speller and because misspelling can seriously detract from the content of your essay. And if you consult page 27 in the RTP Seminar handout, listing the importance of errors, you will see that research on the Regents' test confirms that <u>misspelling</u> is considered a two star error on a scale of 0–3.

Personal Spelling List

Before you can begin to improve your spelling, you must know where the trouble lies. What words and what types of words do you misspell and how do you misspell them? To discover where the trouble lies, keep a personal spelling list in your notebook. From every essay, from every other piece of writing you do, record the words you miss. Your instructor may have you write the misspelled form of the word as well as the correct spelling. One of my colleagues asks her students to correctly write the misspelled word ten times. Certainly you need to keep the list on 3/5 or 4/6 cards, so that you can easily look to see if a word has already been entered. A fellow RTP instructor goes one step further and sets aside a class period to have her students transfer each word from the spelling list to a card, then divide it into syllables—with the meaning on the back if necessary. She instructs the student to write these words correctly each day and checks them herself once or twice during the five week period.

You can carry these functional cards with you wherever you go, and you'll be surprised how often you will have a chance to review them. In our hurry-up-and-wait society, you will have the opportunity for studying your spelling cards as you stand in lines, sit in the doctor's/dentist's office, ride on the Marta train, or wait for class to begin. In fact accomplishing something such as improving your spelling can reduce the stress of all that waiting. Let your family help you, too. Give a stack of cards to those who care about you and ask them to quiz you orally. Finally, make a check mark on the card for each time you continue to misspell a word. Get angry at yourself if you find there are three or four checks on a card. Resolve to conquer the spelling of that word once and for all.

Using the Dictionary

Whenever you enter a word in your spelling list, go to your dictionary for the correct spelling. Do not guess; know that you are entering it correctly. And do not just glance at the word, then write it down and forget it. You know already that the method will do no good, since you now have to turn to the dictionary again and again for certain words, without ever learning them. Instead, make intelligent use of the dictionary; it is one of your strongest allies.

a. Syllabic division

Look at the word carefully, syllable by syllable, with particular attention to the syllables you misspell.

b. Pronunciation

Pronounce the word carefully, syllable by syllable, stressing the troublesome part. If you adopt such careful pronunciation as a regular practice when you are checking spelling, you should in time begin to recognize familiar letter-combinations as they recur, and you will begin to be able to predict what combinations may be possible. There is one further way in which careful pronunciation by syllables will help your spelling. If you habitually leave out certain syllables, if you write convience for convenience or rember for remember, you can spot the difficulty readily by pronouncing the troublesome word as you proof your paper. In each of the examples, you would find yourself a syllable short. It would be no great trouble to then insert the missing syllable, particularly if you make use of the erasable pen.

Visual Spelling

a. The Image in Longhand

As you enter the word in your spelling list, correctly spelled and in your own handwriting, look at it. Look at the whole word, but focus your attention particularly on the syllables you misspell. If it is a word that you habitually misspell, this will be the first time you ever saw the word as it should look in your own handwriting. You have seen it frequently in print, but the visual patterns made by a word in print and in your own longhand are quite different things. Fascinate and *fascinate* do not look very much alike, and seeing the word in print a thousand times will do little to make you realize that you have done something wrong if you read over your themes and see *fascinate* on the page.

b. Fixing the Image

Look at the word you have just written (correctly, remember) for a full minute. Now close your eyes and see if you can visualize it. You will not be able to see it as clearly as you can see your own signature, the specimen of your handwriting

you have seen most often, but you should be able literally to see the word. If the image is vague, look at the word again and again until you can see it clearly.

Fixing such a visual image of the correct form will at least help to warn you as you proof your paper, that a given word is wrong, and it may help you to get it right. You already use the method, in an unmethodical sort of way. How many times have you turned to a sheet of scratch paper and tried out various combinations "to see which looks right"? If you have given yourself clear visual images of the correct form of these troublesome words, you can very easily pick out the correct combination.

Finger Spelling

We usually do not realize how much of our spelling is done by our fingers, without much prompting from our brains. When you want to write the conjunction and, for example, you never think a-n-d. You just write and. Again, how often do your thoughts get ahead of your hand? You are writing, say, "I plan to explain my opinion," and the pl of plan gets mixed up with the pl of explain; when you proof, you wonder how on earth you came to write, "I plain my opinion," as if it were your own two-year-old nephew just learning to talk.

In order to teach the muscles and nerves of your fingers to write a word correctly, make them write it correctly. After you have fixed the visual image of the word, practice writing it. Write it out ten or a dozen times. The next day, do it again. Do not try to increase the dosage. If you set out to write the word twenty times or a hundred times instead of ten or a dozen, you will soon cease to concentrate, and your fingers will fool you by reverting to their old habits until you are actually practicing your mistakes. It is better by far to write a word correctly ten times a day for ten days than a hundred times at a single setting.

Memory Aids

In spite of all your efforts to follow these directions diligently, a few words will get by you. There are ways to learn even these words. If you find that certain words are causing trouble again and again, throw your dignity away and invent memory crutches to help you. It doesn't matter how ridiculous they are. In fact, the more ridiculous they are, the easier it will be to remember them. The pun involved in "The cemetery is full of ease" may be painful, but that pain will keep you from writing cemetery with an a. "The end of friend is end" may make little sense, but it will help you spell friend. "There is a rat in separate" may be sheer nonsense. What of it? It is useful. The word lice may help you remember the li of relieve and believe and the ce of receive, conceive, perceive. Think of ways to remind yourself that a lot are two separate words as are all right. Concentrate on the most troublesome pairs and triplets—accept, except, affect, effect, it's, its, loose, lose, quiet, quite, who's, whose, you're, your and especially their, there, they're and to, too, two.

Regular Patterns

It was suggested earlier that most words are spelled according to their sounds, as those sounds are represented by limited letter-combinations which follow regular patterns.

a. Final consonants before suffixes

In such words as <u>rate</u>, <u>secede</u>, <u>stripe</u>, <u>rope</u>, <u>brute</u>, the long vowel is followed by a single consonant and a silent <u>e</u>. When the <u>e</u> is dropped before certain suffixes, the vowel remains long and the consonant remains single, as in <u>rating</u>, <u>seceded</u>, <u>striping</u>, <u>ropy</u>, <u>brutish</u>.

Short-vowel sounds often occur before single consonants without the final, silent <u>e</u>, as in <u>brag</u>, <u>bed</u>, <u>drip</u>, <u>drop</u>, <u>rut</u>. Followed by vowels, as in many suffixes, the consonants are usually doubled: <u>bragging</u>, <u>bedding</u>, <u>dripping</u>, <u>dropped</u>, <u>rutted</u>.

b. <u>un-</u>, <u>dis-</u>, <u>mis-</u>

Such common prefixes as <u>un</u>, <u>dis</u>, <u>mis-</u> do not affect the spelling of the root word to which they are added. There is one <u>s</u> in *dis-*, one initial <u>s</u> in <u>satisfy</u>, and the two, joined, provide a double <u>s</u>: <u>dissatisfy</u>. But <u>appear</u> has no <u>s</u>, so when <u>dis-</u> is added, only one <u>s</u> is needed: <u>disappear</u>. The same principle applies to <u>unnatural</u>, <u>unappetizing</u>, <u>misspell</u>, <u>mistake</u>.

c. <u>ly</u>, <u>-ness</u>

Such suffixes as <u>-ly</u>, or <u>-ness</u> are simply added to the root. The chief trouble-maker is <u>-ly</u>. Does the root word end in <u>l</u>? If so, when you add <u>-ly</u>, you will have two <u>l</u>'s as in <u>real + ly</u> = <u>really</u>, <u>cool + ly</u> = coolly, and so on. Similarly, <u>barren</u> + <u>ness</u> = <u>barrenness</u>.

d. Plurals

Do plurals bother you? We usually add on <u>s</u> to the singular: <u>boy</u>—<u>boys</u>. If the singular ends in <u>s</u> (or <u>z</u>) sound, or in a <u>ch</u>, <u>sh</u>, or <u>dg</u> sound, we add a syllable when we pronounce the plural, and we spell it <u>-es</u>: <u>classes</u>, <u>matches</u>, <u>brushes</u>, <u>judges</u>.

When a noun ends in <u>y</u> preceded by a consonant, we change the <u>y</u> to <u>i</u> and add -es; lady—ladies, baby—babies. When a noun ends in <u>o</u>, we usually add <u>-es</u>: hero—heroes, potato—potatoes, tomato—tomatoes. (Be careful to remember why the <u>e</u> appears. Do not pull it back into the singular and write heroe or potatoe.) There are many nouns ending in <u>o</u>, however, which add only <u>-s</u>. They are likely to be musical terms from Italian sources, like sopranos, pianos, solos; but there are some others, like silos. Remember that your visual image of the word or a memory crutch may be the most helpful in this regard.

Spelling Rules

Last in the devices which will help you improve your spelling are the "rules." They are like the regular patterns in spelling we have just been considering in that they indicate what usually happens in certain common spelling situations. They are unlike them in that they are extremely, even excessively, familiar to you, and so far they may not have helped very much. But if you really try to use them, they will help a great deal. Actually only about half a dozen of the rules are really helpful. You have seen them often before, but this time, perhaps, you mean business. <u>The following six rules are the most useful.</u>

a. **Ie and ei**

When a word with <u>ie</u> or <u>ei</u> is pronounced with a long <u>e</u>, the most frequent form is <u>ie</u>, The <u>ei</u> usually follows a soft <u>c</u>. You know the rhyme:

I before <u>e</u>
Except after <u>c</u>

Use it. There are nine fairly common exceptions that can be put into a sentence of sorts: <u>Neither financier could inveigle the sheik to seize either species of weird leisure.</u>

If the word is pronounced any other way than a long <u>e</u>, the spelling is usually <u>ei</u>. Some examples of words pronounced other ways: <u>weight</u>, <u>neighbor</u>, <u>counterfeit</u>, <u>foreign</u>, <u>reign</u>. Some use the <u>a</u> sound to remind them of the exception and continue the rhyme:

I before <u>e</u>
Except after <u>c</u>
Or in sounds of <u>a</u>,
like <u>neighbor</u> and <u>weigh</u>.

b. Doubling final consonants

When a word ends in a single consonant preceded by a single vowel, with the accent on the final syllable (or on the syllable, if there is only one), the final consonant is doubled before a suffix beginning with a vowel

<u>strip + ing = stripping</u>
whip + ed = whipped

The rule is important. Every sentence has at least one verb, and by far the greater number of our verbs form their past tenses and past participles by adding -ed. All of them form their present participles and their gerunds by adding -<u>ing</u>. So those two endings alone, or verbs alone, bring this rule into play over and over. And other forms occur, as in

<u>begin—beginner</u>   <u>occur—occurrence</u>
<u>bid—bidder</u>   <u>quiz—quizzes</u>

Remember the rule applies only to words of one syllable or to words accented on the last syllable. If the accent falls earlier, or if the accent shifts to an earlier syllable when the prefix is added, the final consonant is <u>not</u> doubled. Thus:

<u>be'nefit, be'nefited</u>
<u>prefér, preférred,</u> but <u>préference</u>

c. Final silent <u>e</u> before consonants

When a word ends in silent <u>e</u>, retain the <u>e</u> when adding a suffix beginning with a consonant, as in <u>achievement</u>, <u>arrangement</u>, <u>completely</u>, <u>desperately</u>.

Some common exceptions are:

<u>argument</u>, <u>awful</u>, <u>probably</u>, <u>truly</u>, <u>wholly.</u>

d. Final silent _e_ before vowels

When a word ends in silent _e_, drop the _e_ when adding a suffix beginning with the vowel, as in achieving, arranging, completing.

Some exceptions:

•After a soft _c_ or g before _a_ or _o_, as in advantageous, courageous, noticeable.

•To prevent mispronunciation or confusion with other words as in hoeing, shoeing, dyeing, singeing.

e. Consonant plus _y_ before -es or -ed.

Words ending in a consonant plus y change the _y_ to _i_ before adding -es or -ed, as in

> Nouns: baby, babies, city, cities
> Verbs: dry, dries, try, tried

The _y_ also changes to _i_ before some other suffixes, as in happy, happiness, duty, dutiful, dutiable.

f. SEED words

Words that end in the sound SEED usually spell the final syllable -cede, as in concede, precede, recede, secede.

Three words use -ceed: exceed, proceed, succeed. One word uses -sede: supersede.

Words That Sound Alike

RTP students have particular problems with certain words that sound alike but mean different things. These words are spelled differently and are used differently in sentences. For instance, "there" sounds like "their." But "their" means "belonging to them"; "there" means "in a certain place." (Do you see "here" in "there" to give you a clue to its meaning as location and its spelling?) Another word can sound like these two—"they're," the contraction for "there are." Our first set of sound-alikes now includes three words:

> there   their   they're

Another set of words can present problems in spelling:

> to   too   two

"Two" is a number, and it indicates how many objects are in question:

> I have two brothers.

"To" is a preposition. It can introduce phrases of several sorts, but most often it means "toward" or "until." And it is used in verbals like "to scream."

> They took the train to Italy to see Rome.
> We always walked to church.
> He sailed to the north during the storm.

The final member of this set of "sound-alikes" is very clear. "Too" means "also" or "very."

> Mary wants to go too. (Mary wants to go also.)
> He asked for too much. (meaning "very," "excessive amounts")

I like to tell my students that too means to(o)—an extra "o" of something, and I sound it out t-o-o. The sound effects seem to help.

Another pair of words often gets confused: "affect" and "effect." "Effect" is almost always used as a noun to mean <u>end result</u>. Therefore if you want the "e"nd result, the "e"ffect ties in nicely as a reminder. Another "e" reminder requires your asking yourself if you can put "the" before "affect" or "effect" in a sentence. If you can, always use "effect" (th<u>e</u> <u>e</u>ffect-"e" 's go together).

"Affect" is most often a verb meaning "to alter" or "to change"—notice how the "a's" go together—"<u>a</u>"lter = "<u>a</u>"ffect.

> The death of her close friend <u>affected</u> her greatly.
> Smoking <u>affects</u> your lungs and heart.
> My announcement produced an immediate <u>effect</u>.
> Smoking has an <u>effect</u> on the lungs and heart.

"Accept" and "except" are really very different words, but they too get confused. "Accept" is a verb meaning to receive something willingly or to admit to a group. "Except" can be a preposition, a conjunction (a joining word), or a verb. As a preposition, it means "all but," and as a verb it means "to exclude." As a conjunction, we can substitute for "except" the phrase "were it not for the fact that" (you can see that except is shorter and more direct). Check the various meanings and uses in these sentences.

> I <u>accept</u> your gift.
> I was <u>accepted</u> at Clifford College last month.
> Everyone came <u>except</u> Joan.
> In the 1800's, clubs often <u>excepted</u> woman.
> All was well <u>except</u> that the baby was still crying.

Exercises on "Sound Alikes"

Test your understanding of these "sound-alikes":

The right to bare arms.

(Accept/Except) for Mike everyone (accepted/excepted) the offer.

The problem is that (their/they're) coming as a large group.

The (too/two) of us must decide or not (to/too) go, (to/too/two).

(Their/There) go (to/two/too) of my best friends.

I'm not sure (their/there/they're) mother is happy that (their/there/they're) going to study abroad next year.

Each candidate (accepted/excepted) the nomination gratefully (accept/except) Tom Smith.

Gloomy weather has a noticeable (affect/effect) on people's moods.

(Their/There) should be (to/too/two) dozen cookies in the jar.

When the (affect/effect) of inflation becomes clear, it (affects/effects) the consumer buying habits.

THE BIG FOUR

On page **27** of "The Regents Test Preparation Seminar" handout is a ranking of the importance of errors on the Regents' test. In the previous pages of this section on grammar, considerable attention has been paid to identifying and correcting spelling errors which are labeled as less serious but more difficult to avoid. Now it is time to address the <u>big four</u> that composition students seem to think English teachers mumble over and over in their sleep—or should I say their nightmares.

Frag/CS/RO/ are the symbols which identify the most serious errors not only because they distract the English teacher and detract from the content of your essay but also because they indicate your inability to understand what constitutes a complete thought. The SV/agr symbol which identifies subject/verb disagreement has been added to the major error list because raters feel that students getting a degree from the Georgia University System should be able to make nouns and verbs agree in number.

The question of how many of these errors you can make and still pass the Regents' essay test is revealed in the definition of an essay rated "2" or passing: "Although the essay may contain a few serious grammatical errors and several mechanical errors, they are not of sufficient severity and frequency to obscure the sense of what the writer is saying" (p. 19). In other words, if your errors prevent the rater from clearly understanding the meaning of your writing, you will receive a failing or a "1" rating. You may want a clearer definition of what constitutes a passing essay, but it is to your advantage that the criterion is not more specific. Furthermore, since the raters are rated on their consistency with the system average and given a report card on their performance, you can be assured that English professors take their grading job seriously. You are urged to do likewise by keeping a notebook of your Frag/CS/RO/Agr/ errors. Remember studying your errors makes RTP a personalized grammar course.

Eliminating Fragments

The sentence fragment creates a problem for the raters because they expect to see complete thoughts punctuated as sentences. The sentence fragment is an incomplete idea. It can lack a subject, a verb, both subject and verb, or "independence." Look at the following examples which lack components necessary for a complete sentence:

Lacking subject: Ran into the house.
Lacking complete verb: Humans being the most common species.
Lacking subject and verb: Swimming downstream.
Lacking "independence": Which shows the function of a computer.

Obviously, one easy way to proof for sentence fragments is to look at each group of words beginning with a capital letter and ending with a period. If each group has a subject and verb and expresses a complete thought that can stand alone, then it is a sentence and not a sentence fragment. Certainly checking each sentence is time consuming and sometimes frustrating, particularly in the constraints of one hour. A more efficient way to eliminate fragments is to know when they are more likely to occur and to check for them in those situations. Fragments are most common in the introductory paragraph of the Regents' test—before you feel the creative flow—and in the conclusion as you are rushing to complete your essay. Let's be even more specific and deal with each of the fragment "types" in order:

The Fragment without a Subject

The sentence fragment missing a subject will occur when a writer finds a sentence that is too long and divides it into two or more sentences. A sentence can be of any length, but since sentences separate ideas for readers and the myth of "keeping it simple" on the Regents' test prevails, writers start feeling uncomfortable if the sentence goes beyond eight to twenty-five words. Thus, a writer who is under pressure to produce five–seven sentences might be tempted just to put in periods and capital letters not only to keep it simple but also to break up the sentence. He jumped over the fence when he heard the shot. Ran across the backyard. And ran into the house. In haste, the writer has created a sentence and two sentence fragments. A writer who breaks up long sentences to create shorter ones must be careful to provide subjects for all verbs.

The Fragment without a Complete Verb

The fragment missing a subject is less common than the fragment missing a complete verb. The most common fragment error involving an incomplete verb occurs with an "-ing" ending on the main verb. Very often writers will forget that with the "-ing" form they must include some form of "to be" other than "being"; in other words, they must include a "helping word" with the verbal.
Look at the following "sentences":

The water running though the pipes.
The tears streaming down her face.
The television blaring in the empty room.

111

In each case above the "-ing" form of the verb is a verbal, that is, a verb changed so that it does not act as a verb but acts as a modifier of some other part of the sentence. A writer who mistakes a verbal for a complete verb only begins the sentence but does not complete the idea or action of the sentence. Look at the same sentences after a form of "to be" or a "helping word" is added to the verb.

The water <u>is</u> running through the pipes.
The tears <u>were</u> streaming down her face.
The television <u>has been</u> blaring in the empty room.

Verbals are very useful in adding extra information or details to sentences. However, when using verbals, writers must always be sure that the sentence contains a complete verb. "He being impossible" is not a complete sentence, but "He <u>is</u> being impossible" is complete.

The Fragment without Subject or Verb

Like the fragment without a complete verb, the fragment missing both subject and main verb usually involves a verbal—an "-ing" word. Very often, we use verbals at the beginning sentences to explain how the subject of the sentence is doing something or what it is doing. By putting a period after this phrase, a writer can create a fragment that has neither subject nor main verb.

Swimming downstream.
Running quickly down the final stretch.

We can easily change such fragments simply by completing the idea, or, very often, by attaching the fragment to the sentence that comes <u>after it</u> or <u>before it</u>.

Swimming downstream, the boy quickly caught the floating Frisbee.
Jim won the race, running quickly down the final stretch.

Always check any sentences beginning with an "-ing" form to be sure the sentence contains both a subject and a complete verb. If not, attach it to a complete sentence.

The Fragment without "Independence"

Only a complete thought or idea can stand alone as a sentence. When writers punctuate <u>dependent clauses</u> as sentences, they confuse raters, who look for only <u>independent clauses</u> as sentences. By far the most common fragment of all is the fragment caused by punctuating a dependent clause as a sentence. A dependent clause must attach to an independent or main clause so that readers can see the relationships between the dependent and independent ideas. If the dependent clause is not attached to the independent clause it depends on, then readers can become confused about relationships in the paragraph, as in this example:

He became sick. <u>After he took the pill.</u> He later felt better.

Did the pill make him sick, or did it make him feel better? Without the correct punctuation that connects the dependent clause underlined with its main clause, readers cannot understand the ideas expressed. Remember that the definition of a passing Regents' essay is one in which errors are "not of sufficient severity . . . to obscure the sense of what the writer is saying" (p. 19). In this case, the meaning is not clear, and the raters may fail the essay, particularly if several fragments are included.

Certain types of words introduce dependent clauses. The words fall into two categories—those that replace a word in the independent clause ("who," "which," "that," "whose,") and those that "hook" the dependent clause to the independent clause by showing a logical relationship ("after," "before," "when," "where," "since," "because," "although"). We can begin sentences with words from either category. When the sentence begins with "Who," "Whose," "Which," "That," or "Whom," the writers looking for fragments need only check to see if the sentence is a question. If the sentence begins with a word from the second category, then the writers must proof to see that an independent clause follows or precedes the dependent clause. Attaching the dependent clause to a complete thought is the most common way of correcting a fragment error. Remember; if you are interested in using the "although clause" in your thesis, you must attach it to the main clause, or you will lose much or your "although clause" advantage.

ELIMINATING COMMA SPLICES AND RUN-ONS

Let's discuss briefly how we can combine independent clauses within single sentences. Since the independent clause can stand alone, we need to indicate to readers that we have included two or more independent clauses in one sentence. The most common way to combine two or more main clauses is to link them with a coordinating conjunction. Only six words can be coordinating conjunctions ("linking words") that indicate the elements being joined are equally important. These six words are "and," "but," "or," "nor," "for," and "yet." Sometimes "so" can be a coordinating conjunction, but only when it does not mean "so that."

When we use coordinating conjunctions to join two independent clauses, we also use a comma to show that the two connected parts are both independent clauses.

| Independent clause,
(IC) | and
but
or
for
nor
yet
(so) | independent clause.
(IC) |

But remember that independent clauses must have something to connect them, and the link must be more than simply a comma. A semicolon (;) correctly links two independent clauses, or writers can use both a coordinating conjunction and a comma. If you use no punctuation and no coordinating conjunction, you create a run-on (RO) because you have run together two independent clauses. If you use only a comma, you create a comma splice (CS) because you have used a comma to splice or join two independent clauses. Both of these errors are serious because they confuse readers, who must mentally separate the ideas you have joined incorrectly. Again these two errors like the fragment indicate that you do not have understanding of what constitutes a complete thought. Therefore Regents' raters rank these two serious errors among the big four that can most frequently cause a failure or a "1" rating.

Graphic Summary of Punctuation

Let's graphically summarize the <u>correct</u> punctuation this way:

IC = <u>Independent Clause</u>

<u>Correct</u> punctuation between clauses can be:

<u>   IC   </u> .   <u>   IC   </u> .

<u>   IC   </u> , and <u>   IC   </u> .
       (or any coordinating conjunction)

<u>   IC   </u> ; <u>   IC   </u> .

<u>Do not use</u> the following punctuation between independent clauses:

<u>   IC   </u> , (CS) <u>   IC   </u> . (comma splice—a major error)
(Independent clause)   (Independent clause)

<u>   IC   </u> (RO) <u>   IC   </u> . (Run-on—a major error)
(Independent clause)   (Independent clause)

Complicating the punctuation of these complete thoughts is the use of <u>conjunctive adverbs</u> and <u>transitional expressions</u> between independent clauses. These words also provide connections and show relationships between ideas, but because they are not pure connectives and do not have fixed positions, they require the use of a semicolon

(;) between complete thoughts.

<u>Independent clause</u>; conjunctive <u>Independent clause</u>.
            adverb or transitional expression, comma optional

Conjunctive Adverbs and Transitional Expressions

<u>Conjunctive Adverbs</u>

also	incidentally	next
anyway	indeed	nonetheless
consequently	instead	otherwise
finally	likewise	still
furthermore	meanwhile	then
hence	moreover	therefore
however	nevertheless	thus

<u>Transitional Phrases</u>

after all	even so
as a result	for example
at any rate	in addition
at the same time	in fact
by the way	in other words

Remember that conjunctive adverbs and transitional expressions can be picked up and moved to several other spots in the sentence as it suits your fancy. Let's use <u>however</u>, a common conjunctive adverb, as an example. You could write:

The demonstrators have a valid point; <u>however</u>, I can't condone their violence.

<u>or</u>

The demonstrators have a valid point; I can't, <u>however</u>, condone their violence.
<u>or</u> I can't condone their violence, <u>however</u>.

or even

I, <u>however</u>, can't condone their violence.

You will not be able to take such liberties with coordinating conjunctions; you can't move them around. However, it's easy to tell the difference between pure conjunctions (coordinating conjunctions) and conjunctive adverbs if you have memorized the seven coordinating conjunctions: <u>and</u>, <u>but</u>, <u>or</u>, <u>for</u>, <u>nor</u>, <u>yet</u>, <u>(so)</u>. Other connecting words likely to deceive you into thinking they are coordinating conjunctions are actually conjunctive adverbs or transitional expressions.

<u>Test your understanding of Frag/CS/RO errors by completing the exercise on the next page</u>. Don't be surprised if you are able to see the errors in these sentences and groups of words but still have problems with identifying the Frag/CS/RO errors in your practice Regents' essays. You are totally involved with your own writing and often don't recognize the errors. That is why it is so important to let your writing cool as long as possible so that you become your own critic. Since you do not have that luxury in a Regents' test, three suggestions may help you.

Three Suggestions for Eliminating Frag/CS/RO

1. Keep a notebook of the Frag/CS/RO errors in your practice Regents' essays. Analyze when they are most likely to occur and under what circumstances.

2. If you have allotted at least ten minutes for proofing, close your eyes for a couple of minutes after you have written your practice Regents' essays. This practice will not only relax you but also place some distance between you and your writing so that you can more readily spot your errors.

3. If you follow the first two suggestions, you will be able to apply your expertise to the actual Regents' test. You will be in charge of your own writing.

EXERCISES FOR FRAG/CS/RO IDENTIFICATION

Identify each word group, using the following letters:

CS = comma splice; Frag = fragment; S = sentence; RO = run-on

1. A child who was given everything he wanted.   1. _F_

2. Informality is sometimes a good thing; however, it can be carried too far.   2. _CS_

3. Which was not as difficult as I had expected.   3. _F_

4. The owner of a car should, therefore, always carry insurance.   4. _S_

5. The crippled plane was rapidly losing altitude; therefore, the crew tossed all the cargo overboard.   5. _CS_

6. In comparison with most large cities of our country.   6. _F_

7. Even after some motorists install safety belts, they neglect to use them.   7. _S_

8. Mr. Brady is a very unusual person, he listens while other people talk.   8. _CS_

9. They were very nice people, the kind you might meet in any small town.   9. _S_

10. Magnesium, a metal even lighter than aluminum.   10. _F_

11. Your vote is important it decides who runs your government.   11. _RO_

12. Although Milford does a lot of bragging, nobody is the least impressed.   12. _S_

13. A valuable lesson in life which I have never forgotten.   13. _F_

14. Among some letters in an old trunk in our attic.   14. _F_

15. Bruce had to help his family; otherwise, he would have become a doctor.   15. _CS_

16. From early in the morning until late at night.   16. _F_

17. Standing in the doorway, I was protected from the driving rain.   17. _S_

18. It was a few days before Christmas; consequently, the stores were crowded.   18. _RO_

19. The kind of child that only a mother could love.   19. _F_

20. The reporter toured the state, talking with all kinds of people.   20. _S_

116

21. Pretending to agree with Grant, I avoided an unpleasant argument.   21. S

22. The usual procedure in all such cases in billing.   22. F

23. Although some words are considered synonyms, there are usually shades of difference in their meanings.   23. S

24. The ending of the story is unusual, it surprises most readers.   24. CS

25. Where we saw the process of refining oil.   25. F

26. An animal that lived in prehistoric times.   26. F

27. The first movie with spoken dialogue was The Jazz Singer, which was put out by Warner Brothers in 1927.   27. S

28. Some children are stimulated by their parents; consequently, they learn to read early.   28. CS

29. Until we know all the facts, we should keep our minds open.   29. S

30. A job for which he had been well prepared.   30. F

31. From the United States and from many foreign countries.   31. F

32. We raced across the lake, covering ten miles in a half hour.   32. S

33. There was a scratch on the fender, otherwise, the car looked good as new.   33. RO

34. Nash had a prison record; therefore, he had trouble finding a job.   34. CS

35. A new student who was eventually to become my best friend.   35. F

36. The king is merely a figurehead, he has no actual power.   36. CS

37. The brakes and steering, therefore, should frequently be checked.   37. S

38. Especially the blighted area along the riverfront.   38. F

39. A dramatic story told with much skill and power.   39. F

40. Northwest Passage is not a history book. It is a historical novel.   40. RO

41. Mr. Curtis had a low voice; consequently, we plan to use a microphone.   41. RO

42. Inflation raises prices; furthermore, it can lead to an economic crash.   42. CS

ELIMINATING ERRORS IN SUBJECT/VERB AGREEMENT

More than in the study of any other big four error, writers need to memorize a list of rules to conquer their subject/verb agreement problems. A lucky few may have heard the English language used correctly daily in their formative years so that they naturally hear the error—for them it sounds like the wrong note in a piece of music. But for the majority of writers, the following rules will remind them of what their English teachers have told them through the years. And what is more, understanding and following the rules can solve most of the writer's SV/Agr problems.

THE MAJOR RULE IS THAT A VERB AGREES WITH ITS SUBJECT IN NUMBER, WHATEVER THE SUBJECT IS AND WHEREVER IT IS LOCATED.

Twelve Rules to Follow

1. When a word refers to one thing, it is singular in number. When a word refers to more than one thing, it is plural in number.

   a. plural   plural
      subject   verb
      Artichokes   **are** a struggle to eat.
   b. singular   singular
      subject   verb
      An artichoke   **is** a struggle to eat.

2. The number of the subject is not changed by a prepositional phrase or constructions (such as, together with, in addition to, including, as well as) following the subject.

   a. The silhouette of the mountains **looms** against the evening sky.
   b. Monday, as well as the remaining days of the week, **begins** very early in the morning.

3. The following common indefinite pronouns are singular: each, either, neither, one, everyone, everybody, no one, nobody, anyone, anybody, someone, somebody. Everyone has done his/her work promptly.

   To avoid awkwardness in the pronouns that follow the use of such singular, indefinite pronouns and in the spirit of using non-sexist language, many writers are substituting plural nouns for the list above.

   The students **have done** their work promptly.

4. The following common indefinite pronouns are plural: several, few, both, many. Some, any, none, all and most may be either plural or singular.

   a. None of them **deserves** the credit.
   b. None but the brave **deserve** the medals.

5. Compound subjects joined by and are plural and take a plural verb.

   a. Marjorie and Lois **were** glad to see each other again.
   b. Hard work and a little luck **make** for success.
      Some writers find that treating subjects joined by and the same as the pronoun they is helpful in correcting their SV/agr problems.

6. Singular subjects joined by <u>or</u> or <u>nor</u> take a singular verb. When <u>two subjects</u>, one of which is singular and the other plural, are joined by <u>or</u>, <u>nor</u>, the verb agrees with the <u>nearer</u> word.

    a. Either the president or the <u>courts</u> **have** jurisdiction.
    b. Either the courts or the <u>president</u> **has** jurisdiction.

Again some writers like to find a pronoun that matches the one closest to the verb to solve their agreement problems.

7. When the subject and the predicate nominative (subjective complement) are of different numbers, the verb agrees with the subject, not with the predicate nominative (subjective complement).

The only <u>drawback</u> to the apartment <u>is</u> the neighbors' noisy children.

8. When the subject comes after the verb, as in the sentences beginning with <u>here is</u>, <u>there is</u>, <u>where is</u>, be especially careful to determine the subject and make sure that it and the verb agree.

Where **are** my <u>socks</u>?
There **is** one <u>sock</u>.
Here **is** the other <u>sock</u>.

9. Collective nouns may be singular or plural, depending on whether the writer is thinking of the group as a unit or the individual members of the group.

    a. Singular: The <u>board</u> of directors <u>decides</u> all policies.
    b. Plural: The <u>board</u> of directors <u>vote</u> themselves extra fees for every bit of extra work they do.

10. Words stating amount (time, money, measurement, weight, volume, fractions) and some nouns plural in form but singular in meaning—all express singular ideas and take singular verbs.

    a. <u>Two weeks</u> **is** the normal vacation period in business.
    b. <u>Two-thirds</u> of the crop **is** ruined.
    c. <u>Mathematics</u> **is** a confusing subject.
    d. The <u>news</u> **is** good tonight.

11. The title of a song, play, movie, novel, or article, even when plural in form, takes a singular verb.

<u>The Carpetbaggers</u> was made into a movie.

"Stylistic Problems and Their Solutions" is a chapter in the new composition text.

12. If the subject is a relative pronoun, the verb agrees with the antecedent of the pronoun.

    a. He is one of the men <u>who</u> **are** always too tired to work. (The logical relation of the ideas can be seen more readily if the sentence is rearranged: Of those <u>men</u> **who** are always too tired to work, he is one.)
    b. He is the only <u>one</u> of those men <u>who</u> **is** not always tired. (In this sentence, the adjective clause modifies the singular <u>one</u>: Of those men, he is the one who is not always tired.)

Helpful Reminders

Memorizing these rules and applying them in your practice Regents' essays will allow you to take control of your writing. But for RTP students who have frequent problems with SV/Agr there are reminders that are the most useful of all. With most nouns you add an "-s" to make the plural. But with most verbs, the singular form ends in "-s", and you drop it to form the plural:

IF THE SUBJECT HAS AN "S" ENDING BECAUSE IT IS PLURAL,
THEN THE VERB WILL NOT HAVE AN "S" ENDING.
TWO "S" ENDINGS NEVER GO TOGETHER.

Apply your understanding of these SV/Agr rules to this exercise. But once more, remember that it is not your ability to correctly complete this list of sentences that will be the most helpful in solving your problems with subject/verb agreement. Your personalized grammar notebook of errors is the most effective way of correcting this big four error. Taking charge by proofing for those SV/Agr errors you most frequently make will empower you and take away much of your anxiety about subject/verb agreement. Then go one step further and practice the correct subject/verb agreement forms on your friends and family. (Be prepared for some strange looks, for we have informalized SV/Agr as we have no other area of grammar.) Work the standard English patterns into your everyday conversation and gradually your nervous system will take over and you, too, will hear the music and identify the wrong note.

Exercises in Subject-Verb Agreement

1. The welfare of these children (depends, depend) on your generosity. ____

2. The best feature of this magazine (are, is) the pictures of important news events. ____

3. The sweater, as well as the skirt, (was, were) imported from Paris. ____

4. There (is, are) no living organisms in Great Salt Lake except brine shrimps and certain algae. ____

5. It's one of those accidents that (happen, happens) when you're over-tired. ____

6. Rain or snow (don't, doesn't) stop a football game. ____

7. How much (is, are) those leather wallets that you have in the show-case? ____

8. The footprints under the window (suggest, suggests) burglary. ____

9. Tracy Avenue is the only one of our streets that (runs, run) from one end of the city to another. ____

10. The preparations for such a trip (require, requires) much planning. ____

11. The owner or his friends (plan, plans) to use the boat this afternoon. ____

12. The main floor and the balcony (were, was) sold out the first day. ____

13. A ring of mountains (surround, surrounds) the city. ____

14. The heat and the humidity (make, makes) vegetation thrive. ____

15. Richmond or Central High always (win, wins) the city finals. ____

16. Shucking corn and feeding the chickens (was, were) a novelty to us children. ____

17. Every one of the officers of our club (was, were) reelected. ____

18. Neither the students nor the teacher (likes, like) the new textbook. ____

19. There (are, is) about seventy languages spoken in Russia. ____

20. Illness or an emotional disturbance often (affect, affects) one's score on an intelligence test. ____

21. The shift from public transportation to private cars (have, has) caused serious traffic problems. ____

22. The gentleness of these dogs (makes, make) them excellent pets. ____

23. Neither the city nor its suburbs (has, have) an adequate water supply. ____

24. One of the greatest worries of fruit growers (are, is) the early frost. ____

25. One or two short stories (appear, appears) in each issue of our magazine. ____

Entertain your reader with ideas—
not with broad or implied or confusing reference.

"I was told that billions of germs live on one's skin and that they should, therefore, bathe frequently."

"Little by little, she learned to help her mother with a number of household tasks; she even mopped up the floor with her."

Vague Reference   Ref

Your pronoun references should be clear.

"In salt-water trout fishing, the fish are caught either standing on the beach or standing on a pier."

Dangling Modifier   DM

A phrase must have a specific word to modify.

PART VII

APPENDIX

APPROVED REGENTS' TEST ESSAY TOPICS

1. Discuss the influence that advertising has had on your life or the lives of your friends.

2. If you were asked to make a fair evaluation of your teachers, what criteria or standards would you use for the evaluation? Discuss.

3. What influence should students have in the determination of college policies? Explain.

4. Has college made you less sure about what is right and what is wrong? Discuss.

5. How has your attitude toward your home (either town or family) changed between the time you entered college and now? Discuss.

6. If your doctor told you that you had only a few months to live, how would you alter your way of life? Discuss.

7. Name someone you consider to be a modern hero or heroine and explain why you so classify the person.

8. Do college students benefit from participation in extracurricular activities? Explain.

9. Is too much emphasis placed on grades in our educational system? Explain.

10. Each year, many teenagers run away from home. What do you think are the chief causes?

11. Explain why you would or would not want to live in a large city.

12. Should every able-bodied citizen be required to serve for a certain period of time in some branch of the military service? Why or why not?

13. What do you believe are the chief reasons for students' academic failure in college? Explain.

14. How does your public image differ from your private self?

15. How has the automobile been harmful to our society? Explain.

16. If you were an employer, under what circumstances would you fire an employee? Explain.

17. Should sex education be taught in public schools? Why or why not?

18. "Television has made America a nation of watchers, notdoers." Agree or disagree.

19. What are the essential characteristics of an effective leader? Discuss.

20. Do you think that sports help develop good character? Discuss.

21. Explain the chief reasons why students drop out of high school.

22. Should the United States pass gun-control laws? Discuss.

23. Should Georgia legalize gambling to raise more revenue? Discuss.

24. Should Georgia's sales tax be removed from groceries and other necessities? Discuss.

25. Is romantic love a good basis for marriage? Discuss.

26. Should children be disciplined by physical punishment? Discuss.

27. Do you think that you receive your money's worth for your student activity fees? Why or why not?

28. Discuss one cause for which you would be willing to risk your life.

29. Are spectator sports overemphasized in this country today? Discuss.

30. Is college a good place to find out who you really are? Discuss.

31. Discuss the most important characteristics an elected official should have. Why?

32. Do you long for the past or look eagerly toward the future? Explain.

33. Which of the college courses that you have had do you consider to be the most beneficial? Why?

34. Has credit buying affected your way of life? Explain.

35. What changes would occur in your way of life if you were forced to live in a cash economy?

36. Was giving eighteen-year-olds the right to vote a mistake? Discuss.

37. If, in your judgement, the leaders of this country are clearly wrong in adopting a particular policy, what should you do? Explain.

38. If you could have a conversation with a famous person(living or dead), whom would you choose? Discuss.

39. Discuss some practical ways in which each of us can help to conserve natural resources.

40. What steps need to be taken in order to reduce crime? Explain.

41. Do you believe that violence in television programs leads to violence in our society? Explain.

42. Explain your reasons for admiring a particular high school or college teacher.

43. How has the women's liberation movement affected relationships between men and women? Discuss.

44. Which do you think has a greater effect on a person—heredity or environment? Explain.

45. Explain why you do or do not vote.

46. Discuss what could be done to increase the public's respect for police officers.

47. In your opinion, what invention or discovery has brought about the most far-reaching and lasting changes in our civilization? Explain.

48. Should government-owned wilderness areas be preserved? Discuss why or why not.

49. Is it beneficial for a high school graduate to work full-time for a year before entering college? Why or why not?

50. Should the government subsidize our Olympic teams? Why or why not?

51. If you had the power to change any event in history(outcome of an election, who won a war, etc.), which would you choose to change, and why?

52. What characteristics do you regard as important in a person you would choose as a friend?

53. Should both parents assume equal responsibility in child rearing? Explain why or why not.

54. What vice or weakness do you find most offensive? Explain.

55. How great a role do you think "knowing the right people" plays in getting ahead in school or in work? Explain.

56. What are the essential characteristics of a good parent? Discuss.

57. Should court proceedings be televised? Explain why or why not?

58. "American family life would be more stable if parents,not couples involved, arranged marriages." Agree or disagree.

59. Students at public colleges currently pay, through tuition and fees, about one-fourth of the cost of their education; however, some people say students should pay a greater share of the cost. Argue for or against this proposal.

60. Is there any job that you would absolutely refuse to take? Explain.

61. Should government employees such as police officers and fire fighters have the right to strike? Discuss.

62. What advice would you give to an entering freshman? Discuss.

63. Should prostitution be legalized? Discuss.

64. Which courses that you did not take in high school do you now wish you had taken? Why?

65. Research indicates that you and your friends are likely to have fewer children than your parents and grandparents. What do you think are reasons for this? Explain.

66. What makes one college course more enjoyable than another? Explain.

67. Should smoking in public places be illegal? Explain why or why not.

68. "Professional athletes and entertainers are among the highest paid people in this country—and justifiably so."Agree or disagree.

69. What are the characteristics of a good college student? Explain.

70. Should college students have complete freedom to choose their own courses? Discuss.

71. If you were to be deprived of one of your five senses(sight, touch, smell, taste, and hearing) which one would you most hate to give up? Explain.

72. Would you prefer to rear a family in the city or the country? Explain why.

73. In general, do movies and/or television provide a realistic picture of life in America? Explain.

74. How should public high schools deal with students considered to be constant troublemakers? Discuss.

75. Some states now permit single men and women to adopt children. Do you favor such a policy? Explain why or why not.

76. Should college students be required to attend classes? Discuss.

77. For what qualities or achievements would you feel justified in calling an individual successful? Explain.

78. Recent elections have been characterized by small turnouts of eligible voters. Some democracies—Australia, for example—require their citizens to vote. Explain why such a policy should or should not be adopted in the United States.

79. Discuss some of the status symbols of today's society.

80. Various commentators have suggested that no person should serve more than twelve years in either the U.S. Senate or the U.S. House of Representatives. Discuss.

81. Should people on welfare be forced to work? Explain why or why not.

82. Why do you believe radio has continued to be popular in the age of television? Discuss.

83. Should all college courses be specifically related to one's future occupation? Explain why or why not.

84. Many families today are growing home vegetable gardens. Discuss some reasons for this.

85. How can a course in government, political science, or civics help students to become better citizens? Explain.

86. What do you think are the major causes of divorce? Explain.

87. Choose a profession whose members make a worthwhile contribution to society and discuss the benefits that society receives from members of this profession.

88. Discuss ways to increase the public's respect for elected officials.

89. What, in your opinion, are some of the reasons so many people have pets? Discuss.

90. Do you prefer shopping at a large shopping center or at downtown stores? Discuss.

91. Apart from chronological age, what are some major differences between an adolescent and an adult? Explain.

92. Should women in the military services be assigned combat duties? Discuss.

93. Attack or defend the practice of advertising by doctors and lawyers.

94. Discuss what you like or do not like about the South.

95. What do you think would be the consequences of the legalization of marijuana? Explain.

96. Does our society allow women to assume masculine roles more readily than it allows males to assume roles traditionally called feminine? Discuss.

97. If you were made the programming director of a major television network, what changes in the programming would you make? Explain.

98. If you could live in some other historical period, which would you choose, and why?

99. Should fathers be given the same chance as mothers to gain custody of their minor children? Discuss.

100. We now have more people over 65 than at any other time. What are the major effects of this increased proportion of older people? Discuss.

101. Should victims of crime be compensated? Explain.

102. Do you function best in the morning, afternoon, or evening? Explain.

103. What do you think are the major effects of divorce upon children? Discuss.

104. It has been proposed that American presidents be elected for one six-year term and not be eligible for reelection. Do you agree with this proposal? Discuss.

105. Why did you choose the career for which you are preparing?

106. Do you favor increased spending for national defense? Why or why not?

107. Should the United States severely restrict the import of foreign cars for sale in the United States? Discuss.

108. "In spite of advances in scientific knowledge, people are still superstitious." Agree or disagree.

109. Watching the "soaps" has become an American pastime. Why are these television shows so popular?

110. Which is most useful to a college student—a pick-up truck, a car, or a bicycle? Explain.

111. In the United States, as a rule, are the punishments imposed appropriate to the crimes committed? Explain.

112. Why do some couples choose to live together without getting married? Explain.

113. Would you like to be a candidate for public office? Why or why not?

114. Do college students benefit from having to earn at least part of their tuition? Discuss.

115. If music reflects the mood of an age, what does current music say about America? Explain.

116. Are Americans too dependent on the automobile? Discuss.

117. What are the characteristics of an effective television newscaster? Explain.

118. Why are so many people over the age of twenty-one enrolling in college? Discuss.

119. Discuss changes which would make the public less hesitant to report crime.

120. Do Americans seem unable to relax in their leisure time? Discuss.

121. "Human rights" is a term frequently used but seldom defined. What rights should belong to every human being? Discuss.

122. Should American students be required to learn a second language? Why or why not?

123. Do you or your family support public television (the educational channels) either as viewers or contributors? Why or why not?

124. Are elementary and high schools adequately meeting the needs of their students? Discuss.

125. How you account for the popularity of horror films? Discuss.

126. Robert Frost said, "We come to college to get over our little mindedness." Discuss in relation to your own experiences.

127. In what ways has the availability of fast food restaurants affected your eating habits?

128. Because of the high cost of gasoline, many people are using transportation other than the automobile. In your opinion, what other types of transportation are most feasible?

129. What do you hope to accomplish within the next ten years? Explain.

130. Should college students be required to take physical education courses? Why or why not?

131. It has been said that "Evil, like good, has its own heroes." Name some characters that you consider to be "evil heroes." Explain.

132. If you could ban anything in the world, what would it be and why?

133. Should prison inmates be allowed to take college courses? Explain why or why not.

134. If you were awarded an expense paid trip to any one place in the world, where would you go? Why?

135. Do you think that you have the qualifications of a good parent? Discuss.

136. What do you consider the most important event of the past decade? Why?

137. If you were guaranteed a steadily improving standard of living (in terms of buying power, free time, quality of goods and services, etc.), would you be willing to give up your right to vote? Explain.

138. Jogging has become extremely popular in the last few years. Explain why you jog or why you don't.

139. Is it possible for anger ever to be beneficial? Explain.

140. How can the individual citizen reduce the probability of his or her home's being burglarized? Explain.

141. What are the most important skills and/or values that children learn from their parents? Explain.

142. Is it better for a political leader to be feared instead of loved? Why or why not?

143. What specific sacrifice or sacrifices would you endure as a partial solution to our country's economic problem? Discuss.

144. Most people consider themselves part of a particular generation. Discuss what you consider the most important values of your generation.

145. Should a graduating college senior be required to pass a comprehensive examination in his or her major before receiving a degree? Why or why not?

146. Is an academically competitive atmosphere helpful or harmful to you as a student? Discuss.

147. Should the government do more to discourage cigarette smoking? Why or why not?

148. "Manners belong to a bygone age; they are no longer relevant." Attack, defend, or modify.

149. In your view, what would most impress (favorably or unfavorably) a foreign student spending his or her first weekend in an American home? Discuss.

150. At a scientific conference, Russia's chief space scientist, Leonid I. Sedov, taunted a U.S. colleague: "You Americans have a better standard of living than we have. But the American loves his car, his refrigerator, his house. He does not, as we Russians do, love his country." If you had to answer Mr. Sedov, what would be your reply?

151. Discuss the advantages and/or disadvantages of nuclear power as a source of energy.

152. In what areas should all college graduates be required to have some competence? Why?

153. Is marriage an outmoded institution in the United States? Explain why or why not.

154. Is athletic competition good for children under twelve years old? Explain why or why not.

155. Many American homes and offices have become a jungle of houseplants. Why do you think that so many people surround themselves with growing things?

156. If you could make one scientific discovery in your lifetime, what would it be? Why?

157. Given all the evidence that cigarette smoking is harmful, why do people continue to smoke cigarettes? Discuss.

158. If the average life span were increased to 150 years, what major changes in society would you expect? Discuss.

159. What would cause you to end a friendship? Explain.

160. When we return to places we knew as children, we are often surprised at how different these places seem. Compare and/or contrast your impression of some place you knew as a child with your current impression of the same place.

161. Do you believe that banning certain books from public and school libraries is justified? Discuss.

162. Do high schools put too much emphasis on athletics? Discuss.

163. What would you place in a time-capsule to allow people opening the capsule 1,000 years from now to understand life in the 1980's? Explain.

164. "Self-discipline is the most important ingredient for success." Attack or defend.

165. Describe a model physical fitness plan.

166. Does our public educational system promote mediocrity? Discuss.

167. Is it harmful for children to be in day-care centers all day? Explain why or why not.

168. Should the custom of tipping be abolished? Explain why or why not.

169. "In the United States, we waste a great natural resource: the elderly." Agree or disagree.

170. Beauty contests, despite some criticism, are still very popular. In your opinion, what are the chief reasons for their popularity? Explain.

171. What are the chief causes of shoplifting? Discuss.

172. Overcrowded prisons are one of the major problems facing Georgia. What might be done to ease this problem?

173. What can be done to prevent violence and crime in public schools? Discuss.

174. Should law enforcement agencies be permitted to tap telephone lines? Explain.

175. Should public agencies be required to inform parents if their minor children (those under 17) seek birth control? Discuss.

176. If you could pass one law, what would it be? Why?

177. What do you consider to be your duties as a citizen? Discuss.

178. Should national and state governments set aside land for parks? Discuss.

179. Do you believe that it is the responsibility of the young to provide financial security for the aged? Why or why not?

180. Why are many people afraid of growing old? Discuss.

181. What can parents do to prepare their children for school? Discuss.

182. The changes brought on by the women's liberation movement are typically seen as benefiting women. Do men also benefit from women's liberation? Discuss.

183. According to studies, the average American watches television as much as six hours a day. Why do Americans watch so much television? Discuss.

184. America has many regional foods. What would you recommend to a traveler who wanted to experience Southern food? Explain.

185. If you could hold any job for one year, what would you choose? Why?

186. If you could change one thing about your childhood, what would it be? Discuss.

187. How can parents promote good reading habits in their children? Discuss.

188. Is it better to have brothers and sisters than to be an only child? Explain.

189. Is the traditional role of fathers changing? Discuss.

190. It has been said that computers are taking over our lives. Do you agree or disagree? Explain.

191. Is the person without knowledge of computers in the 1990's handicapped? Discuss.

192. Should adoption records be open to the people directly involved (the person adopted, the biological parents and/or the adoptive parents)? Explain why or why not.

193. How does a person make a good first impression in an interview? Discuss.

194. What is your most prized possession? Why?

195. What is your definition of a gentleman or a lady? Explain.

196. What is the value of recreation? Explain.

197. Should teenaged children of divorced parents have the right to decide which parent to live with? Discuss.

198. P. T. Barnum said that "a sucker is born every minute." Explain how this idea relates to American advertising.

199. Should college physical education grades be included in the grade point average? Discuss why or why not.

200. Do you favor or oppose a rule that would prohibit professional teams from recruiting college student athletes until their college sports eligibility is over? Why or why not?

201. Knowledge can be gained from books and scientific observation. What are some other important sources of knowledge, and why are they valuable?

202. Whether we want them or not, many of us get tagged with one or more nicknames during our lives. Discuss the positive and/or negative aspects of the practice of nicknaming.

203. Whom would you identify as a truly wise person? What makes him or her seem wise to you?

204. Archaeologists have learned much about the lives of first-century Romans from the excavations of houses buried by lava at Pompeii. Suppose that your home were preserved just as it is now. What conclusions about life in the 1990's might this evidence lead future archaeologists to draw?

205. Discuss what people reveal about themselves by the way they drive.

206. What steps should be taken to improve the quality of education in our public schools? Discuss.

207. Name your favorite game or sport and explain why you find it enjoyable.

208. What should a college athlete consider in deciding whether to turn professional or to remain in college?

209. Athletic programs at some colleges are big business. Discuss the advantages and/or disadvantages of this situation.

210. Discuss how student evaluations of faculty could be used by administrators, faculty, and/or students.

211. Partners in marriage often write their own detailed marriage contracts, covering such matters as the number of children they wish to have and the management of money. Would you write such a contract? Explain why or why not.

212. In the development of a national budget, which should be more important— fighting poverty at home or arming to fight an aggressor? Explain.

213. Should all students be required to take a course in computer science some time during their education? Explain why or why not.

214. Which of the four seasons of the year appeals to you the most? Why?

215. Suicide among high school and college students is on the rise in this country. Discuss possible reasons why young people take their own lives.

216. What is the best advice you ever got? Explain.

217. Discuss why people are fascinated by amusement parks such as Disney World and Six Flags.

218. Explain why you do or do not hunt.

219. Discuss some of the roles a college student plays.

220. How effective is television in disseminating news? Explain.

221. What steps would you recommend be taken to make health care in America more available to everyone? Explain.

222. Is it better to know a little about many subjects than to know a lot about one subject? Discuss.

223. Should an introduction to art, music, and drama be a part of every college student's education? Explain why or why not.

224. Do you believe young college students should postpone marrying until they graduate? Why or why not?

225. Should cardiopulmonary resuscitation (CPR)/first aid courses be a required part of the college's curriculum? Discuss why or why not.

226. How do you expect your college education to change the rest of your life? Discuss.

227. Should every college student take a course in public speaking? Discuss.

228. What are some possible reasons for the recent decline in the reading skills of high school students? Discuss.

229. What could be done to make students more interested in learning about science? Discuss.

230. Should the law require automobile drivers and passengers to use safety belts? Discuss.

231. Discuss some of the appeals used in automobile advertisements.

232. What steps should be taken to reduce the number of drunk drivers? Discuss.

233. Is increased life expectancy a blessing or a curse? Discuss.

234. Every applicant for a Georgia driver's license must choose whether to be an organ donor. Would you choose to be a donor? Explain why or why not.

235. Should the United States offer foreign aid only to those nations which support our policies? Discuss.

236. Do you support the nuclear freeze movement that has recently gained momentum in both Europe and the United States? Explain why or why not.

237. What is your favorite piece of furniture? Explain.

238. Though a favorite sport of many, boxing is a dangerous sport that leaves many boxers suffering from eye and brain damage. Should it be outlawed?

239. Are large stockpiles of sophisticated military weapons necessary to deter foreign aggression? Discuss.

240. Why do people still go to movie theaters despite the availability of television movies and video cassettes? Discuss.

241. If you were forced to live without television, how would you spend the time you normally spend watching TV? Discuss.

242. How have your eating habits changed since you've been in college? Discuss.

243. Do you think of yourself as a "goal-oriented" person? Explain.

244. Does a person have to be wealthy and powerful in order to be considered successful? Discuss.

245. If you had the power to do one thing to improve the world, what would you do? Discuss.

246. What do you think are the best methods of disciplining children? Explain.

247. If you could have a household robot, for what jobs would you want it programmed? Discuss.

248. Is it the responsibility of the United States to share its food supplies with the hungry people of the world? Explain.

249. What is the value of foreign travel? Discuss.

250. The United States has never had a female president. To what do you attribute this? Discuss.

251. What is the difference between "good" and "bad" stress? Explain.

252. If you could choose any culture or society, which one would you choose to live in? Discuss.

253. Why have the Southern states been gaining population in the last two decades? Discuss.

254. Discuss some of the advantages and/or disadvantages of having two or three generations of a family living together under the same roof.

255. Why do people play practical jokes? Explain.

256. What does it mean to be fully alive? Explain.

257. If you were alone for a week, what books (or music) would you select to read (or listen to)? Discuss.

258. Should teachers be required to pass competency tests? Discuss.

259. What type of music do you prefer? Why?

260. Why is college football so popular? Discuss.

261. Which of your talents do you value most? Why?

262. Do you feel that college professors show favoritism among students? Discuss.

263. Should the school year be extended to include longer hours and more days required to obtain a high school diploma? Discuss.

264. If you were among the first colonizers of a new planet in the twenty-first century, what would you not want your fellow colonists to transport from the planet Earth? Explain.

265. Discuss some of the differences you have noticed between written and spoken language.

266. Americans generally condemn daydreaming as a waste of time. Do you agree with this view, or do you see some benefits of daydreaming? Discuss.

267. When you are approached for a charitable contribution, do you generally contribute? Why or why not?

268. Publishers report that astrology columns are among the most widely read features in newspapers. Do you check your astrological forecast from time to time? Why or why not?

269. The evidence shows that for many reasons the family-owned and family-run small farm is a vanishing American institution. Should this situation cause concern in American society? Why or why not?

270. Do you suppose you would be happier if you lived more simply, eliminating the effort it takes to acquire an abundance of luxuries? Why or why not?

271. Do you read the newspaper every day? Why or why not?

272. The "Living Will' directs a person's family and physicians not to keep that person alive by artificial means if that person were to suffer a totally incapacitating disease or illness. Would you consider signing such a document and giving it to your own family? Why or why not?

273. Is noise pollution becoming a serious threat to the welfare of Americans? Discuss.

274. "Very few of us really know how to listen." Discuss why you agree or disagree with this statement.

275. Is it better to have loved and lost than never to have loved at all? Discuss.

276. "Any teacher who can be replaced by a machine, should be." Discuss why you agree or disagree with this statement.

277. Do you favor or oppose the use of animal organs (such as hearts or kidneys) as transplants in humans when human organs are not available? Explain.

278. The Supreme Court has recently ruled that public schools have the right to conduct searches of students' persons and property when there is reasonable cause to suspect the presence of weapons or drugs. Do you support or oppose such searches? Explain.

279. Would you be better off if you didn't own a television? Discuss.

280. It is said that the United States has the highest crime rate of any country that keeps accurate records. What, in your opinion, are some of the reasons for the unusually high rate of crime in the U.S.? Discuss.

281. If you could participate in only one extra-curricular activity, which would you choose? Why?

282. What measures might be effective in reducing drug traffic in Georgia? Discuss.

283. Should the government allow unlimited numbers of refugees from political oppression to enter the U.S.? Discuss.

284. Should the government cut funds from educational, cultural, and welfare programs to support a strong defense budget? Discuss.

285. Should the advertisement of alcoholic beverages be banned from television? Discuss.

286. Should tax dollars be used to subsidize public television and radio broadcasts? Discuss.

287. If you were placed in a position to reduce the national debt, what area would you cut? Why?

288. Many states have enacted laws banning all non-refundable drink containers. Should Georgia pass such a law? Why or why not?

289. Some think that divorces are too easy to obtain today. Do you agree or disagree? Explain.

290. What steps can be taken to reduce the amount of litter found along highways and in the countryside? Discuss.

291. Should stricter laws be enacted banning billboards along our major highways? Why or why not?

292. Presidential greatness is often debated by professional historians. Which U.S. president would you identify as the greatest? Justify your selection.

293. Several communities have recently passed laws making it illegal for bars to promote the consumption of alcohol through sales specials such as happy hours, two-for-one hours, and ladies' night. Do you agree or disagree that these laws are needed? Discuss.

294. What is your favorite source of entertainment? Explain why.

295. Would you want to survive a nuclear war? Discuss.

296. Is it better to have lived in one place all one's life than to have moved around? Discuss.

297. What is your favorite holiday? Why?

298. Do Americans place too much emphasis on physical appearance? Discuss.

299. Nearly all students have had classmates who they wished were anywhere else but in that particular class. What kinds of students do you find most annoying? Discuss.

300. Should the media show more respect for celebrities' desire for privacy? Discuss.

301. "The best things in life are free." Discuss why you agree or disagree with this statement.

302. Is there anything that teachers can learn from students? Discuss.

303. If you had to choose between a job that you loved that paid $15,000 a year and a job that you hated that paid $30,000 a year, which job would you take? Explain why.

304. Why do so many people like to have collections of something (antiques, coins, stamps, dolls)? Discuss.

305. It has been said that winning is not the most important thing; it's the only thing. Explain why you agree or disagree with this view.

306. With the widespread availability of calculators, is it necessary for students to learn arithmetic? Discuss.

307. Should student evaluations of faculty members be made available to students? Discuss why or why not.

308. Has the space program benefited the average American? Discuss.

309. With news readily available from the electronic media, why are newspapers still popular? Discuss.

310. What are the advantages and/or disadvantages of being single? Discuss.

311. Should parents encourage their teenage children to work even if the family does not need the money?

312. Who is a sex symbol today? Explain.

313. Which advertisements do you find most appealing or offensive? Why?

314. What do you do to cope with stress?

315. Do you think that most people would rather conform (be like everyone else in a group) than stand out as individuals? Discuss.

316. What contemporary problem do you find most disturbing? Explain.

317. Has television brought members of the family together? Discuss.

318. Are robots a blessing or a curse to the labor force? Discuss.

319. What animal do you like (or dislike) the most? Why?

320. Should polygraph tests be used as a condition of employment? Discuss.

321. If you could live in any city in the world, which would you choose and why?

322. What single experience do you believe every human being should have, one without which human life, in your opinion, would not be complete? Explain.

323. Should children diagnosed as having AIDS be permitted to attend public schools? Discuss why or why not.

324. What is the greatest bargain you have ever got? Explain.

325. Should college students be tested for AIDS? Discuss why or why not.

326. Discuss some of the pressures on college students.

327. Should final examinations in college courses be comprehensive? Discuss.

328. Discuss the advantages and/or disadvantages of being a commuting student.

329. If you were a fashion designer for college students on a budget; what wardrobe would you suggest that would be reasonably priced and adaptable to various occasions?

330. Explain what motivates you to strive for good grades in college.

331. Many college freshmen complain that they have never learned how to study. What pointers could you give to help people with poor study habits? Explain.

332. Is it an advantage or a disadvantage to have a job while attending college? Discuss.

333. Should colleges make it optional for students to pay activities fees? Discuss why or why not.

334. What types of students do you like to have in your classes? Discuss.

335. Should computer literacy be required of all college students? Discuss why or why not.

336. Should the government increase taxes to help improve the standard of living of poor people? Discuss why or why not.

337. How do you think our future will be influenced by the great influx of foreign products into the United States? Explain.

338. In order to protect American industry, should the U.S. government impose heavy tariffs on foreign goods coming into this country? Discuss why or why not.

339. Have you observed any significant differences between high school and college teachers? Explain.

340. What advice would you give to a student just beginning high school? Explain.

341. How can we reduce the problem of illiteracy in our nation? Explain.

342. Do American students know far too little about their Russian counterparts? Discuss.

343. Should high school students be required to wear uniforms? Discuss why or why not.

344. What can public schools do to lower the number of high school dropouts? Explain.

345. Should schools establish dress codes? Discuss.

346. Is concern for a clean environment a dead issue today? Discuss.

347. One suggested partial solution to the drug problem is to furnish drugs to certified addicts, thus removing the profit for drug dealers. What do you think of this idea?

348. Should employers have the right to require their employees to take drug tests? Discuss why or why not.

349. Should a person tell his or her spouse about past love affairs? Discuss why or why not.

350. What can be done to help prevent a marriage from ending in divorce? Explain.

351. Would you rather spend a weekend with your friends or your family? Explain.

352. Of the sources of entertainment which are popular today, which do you find least appealing? Discuss.

353. What was the most important event of your life? Discuss why this event was so important.

354. What types of movies do you prefer? Explain.

355. Which do you believe has been most influential in your life—good luck (chance) or good decisions? Explain.

356. Have recent reports on airline crashes and near collisions changed your attitude toward air travel? Discuss why or why not.

357. What impact has attending college had on your relationships with others? Explain.

358. What types of reading materials do you prefer? Discuss.

359. If you could buy one very expensive thing, what would it be? Explain.

360. How do you account for the popularity of your favorite entertainer?

361. What kind of information would you want to obtain before making a major purchase such as a car or stereo system?

362. How would your life change if you inherited a million dollars?

363. Name a person, place, or thing that is currently very popular but that, in your opinion, is overrated. Explain why it does not deserve its popularity.

364. What career, other than the one for which you are preparing, do you find most appealing? Explain.

365. What situations are most stressful for you? Discuss.

366. Discuss the importance that a relative (other than a parent) has had in your life.

367. Given the choice, would you rather live in the mountains or near the beach? Discuss.

368. If you were to set up a personal museum of the most significant objects you own, what would you include and why?

369. Do you like surprises? Explain why or why not.

370. Explain why you do or do not smoke.

371. Discuss a New Year's resolution that you actually kept (or wish you had).

372. What region of the United States do you like the most? Why?

373. If for some reason you were prevented from attending college, what career would you pursue? Why?

374. Explain why you do or do not like having picnics.

375. Is there one place on earth that means more to you than all others? Why?

376. People dress to project an image or to follow trends or to be comfortable. Discuss why you dress the way you do.

377. What have you been promising to throw out for years but just cannot seem to part with? Discuss.

378. If you could relive one day in your life, which day would it be? Explain.

379. What is your idea of a perfect vacation? Explain.

380. What are some characteristics of people you try to avoid when selecting friends? Explain.

381. What would be the ideal number of children for you to have in a family? Discuss.

382. Name some of your family's traditions (perhaps concerning holidays, birthdays, vacations, or other activities) and discuss why they are important to you.

383. How are you different from your parents (or other adults significant in your upbringing)? Explain.

384. Explain why you would or would not recommend a movie you saw recently.

385. What advice would you give to a person about the process of ending a meaningful relationship?

386. What influences from the past have helped shape the person you are today? Discuss.

387. If private ownership of automobiles were impossible, how would your life change?

388. If you could have free, unlimited service for five years from an extremely good cook, chauffeur, housekeeper, masseuse, or personal secretary, which one, if any, would you choose? Why?

389. What foreign country would you like to visit, and why would you like to go there?

390. What can be done to encourage more and better candidates to seek public office? Explain.

391. Has media scrutiny of public officials' private lives become excessive? Discuss.

392. Should local governments pass a law restricting the ownership of dangerous pets such as pit bulldogs? Discuss why or why not.

393. What advice would you give to a young person just beginning to date? Discuss.

394. More and more people are seeking plastic surgery for purely cosmetic reasons. Why are so many people willing to accept the costs and risks of this kind of surgery?

395. Explain why you think so many people get the post-Christmas blues.

396. Are people in the U.S. overly concerned about being thin? Discuss.

397. Americans are fast becoming the most overweight people in the world. To what do you attribute this trend? Explain.

398. Should animals be used in medical research? Discuss.

399. What can be done to improve the treatment of the elderly?

400. What can be done to make the public more aware of the dangers of drinking and driving?

401. What has been the most useless invention of the twentieth century? Explain.

402. Do you think a person's looks affect his or her success in the job market? Discuss why or why not.

403. What should be done to reduce the problem of homelessness in the U.S.?

404. How can Halloween be made safer for young people?

405. Some television series (such as *M.A.S.H.*, *The Andy Griffith Show* and *Leave It To Beaver*) have enjoyed a long life both in production and in reruns. Explain why.

406. What are the chief reasons for our youth's interest in music videos? Explain.

407. Choose a character in a recent movie or television show whom you find especially appealing or unappealing. Explain your choice.

408. Why are television game shows so popular? Discuss.

409. Why do many people prefer watching television news shows over reading newspapers? Discuss.

410. Do you like being in the presence of small children? Discuss why or why not.

411. Should people accept it as their duty to take care of their aging parents? Discuss.

412. Women today are waiting until they are older to marry for the first time. Why?

413. If you could take back any deed you have done and do it differently, what would it be? Why?

414. Fill in the blank in the following statement and discuss: "They don't make _____ like they used to."

415. What commonly held ideas about the South seem to you most true or untrue? Explain.

416. What is the dumbest thing you ever did? Explain why you did it.

417. What kind of injustice makes you "fighting mad"? Explain.

418. How is the threat of AIDS changing dating habits? Explain.

419. Which qualities or characteristics of childhood should we strive to preserve throughout our lives? Discuss.

420. What can be done to reduce the high rate of teenage pregnancy in the United States? Explain.

421. How should students who turn in someone else's work as their own be punished? Discuss.

422. Should high-school students go steady? Discuss why or why not.

423. Name the worst movie or television program you have ever seen, and explain why you dislike it.

424. Is there ever a situation in which a person should hide his or her true feelings? Explain.

425. Name your favorite pastime and explain why you enjoy it.

426. Name some place you would not like to go on a date and explain why you would choose not to go there.

427. Propose a model sex education program.

428. If you could make one resolution and follow through with it no matter what the difficulties, what would you choose? Explain.

429. Are there superstitions you claim you do not believe and yet would never ignore? Explain.

430. Most people agree that for a leader to lead, there must be those who are willing to be led. What does it take for a person to be a responsible follower? Explain.

431. Why are people often unwilling to intervene in or report crimes that they observe? Explain.

432. Has there been a time in your life when you should have complained about a situation but didn't? Discuss.

433. Discuss the images of men presented in recent movies and television shows.

434. Discuss the images of women presented in recent movies and television shows.

435. Discuss the images of children presented in recent movies and television shows.

436. Discuss the images of minorities presented in recent movies and television shows.

437. Would you prefer to attend an amateur or a professional athletic event? Explain.

438. Why do Americans eat so much junk food? Explain.

439. How do you account for the popular appeal of murder mysteries (in novels, movies, and TV dramas)?

440. What elective course that you have taken would you <u>not</u> recommend to other students? Explain your dissatisfaction with the content of the course.

441. Has attending college made you a better person? Discuss.

442. Discuss what you perceive to be some of the causes of homelessness in America.

443. How do you think the money raised by the lottery in Georgia should be spent? Discuss.

444. Discuss the special problems that single parents and their children face.

445. Do you believe that recycling should be mandatory? Discuss.

446. Should physicians be prevented from intentionally providing people with the means to commit suicide? Discuss.

447. Some people have argued that zoos are inhumane, that keeping animals captive is wrong. Discuss why you agree or disagree.

448. Is there one sport that you would never play and/or would never want to play? Explain.

449. Some people have begun to regulate the hours of television that their children may watch each week by giving each child a "television allowance" time. Do you believe that this is a good idea? Why or why not?

450. If you could be a cast member of any movie ever made, which film would you choose? Why?

451. What should be invented, but has not yet been, that would make your life easier? Explain.

452. If you could donate a thousand dollars to a charity, what charity would you choose. Why?

453. Many women in the film industry have for years complained that not enough significant female roles are available for them. Do you agree or disagree? Explain.

454. A character in *Hamlet* says, "Neither a borrower nor a lender be." Is this good advice? Explain.

455. John Kennedy once said, "Ask not what your country can do for you; ask what you can do for your country." Are Americans heeding this call from the past? Explain.

456. Studies over the last twenty years have shown that academic dishonesty is on the rise in colleges across the United States. To what do you attribute this increase in cheating? Explain.

457. Have you observed any significant differences between older and younger college students in classroom discussions? Discuss.

458. If you could influence the way products are advertised in the United States, what recommendations, if any, would you make? Discuss.

459. What are some activities that are especially appealing to children? Why?

460. Should sex education programs emphasize the need for abstinence before marriage? Discuss.

461. What do you think have been the main reasons for the increase in violent behavior in our schools? Explain.

462. Discuss the image of women presented in music videos.

463. What changes might occur if gasoline prices rose to $3.00 a gallon? Discuss.

464. Why are Americans generally resistant to learning foreign languages? Explain.

465. If you had the time and opportunity to sit in on any college classes just for the purpose of learning about the subject, which classes would you choose? Why?

466. Have you ever been pressured into doing something that you would have preferred to avoid but that later turned out to be beneficial? Discuss.

467. Why are movies and television shows about actual crimes so popular today? Discuss.

468. Should a person who has been convicted of a crime be allowed to run for public office? Discuss why or why not.

469. Why is it that political candidates do not always keep their campaign promises once they are in office? Discuss.

470. Should homosexuals be permitted to serve in the military? Discuss why or why not.

471. Is it appropriate for the President of the United States to appoint a close relative to an important policy-making position? Discuss.

472. Have you ever learned something that seemed insignificant at the time but that later became particularly valuable? Discuss.

473. If you could endorse one product that met its advertised claims, what would that product be? Explain.

474. Discuss a stereotype that you once believed but that later proved inaccurate.

475. Should English be the standard language in public schools or should schools be required to offer classes in the language a student speaks at home? Discuss.

476. What things would you look for when buying or renting a place to live? Discuss.

477. What are the advantages and/or disadvantages of growing up in a large family as opposed to a small family? Discuss.

478. Should state governments spend more money on school districts with low-achieving students than on districts with high-achieving students? Discuss.

479. Describe a decision you have made that has been particularly significant to you.

480. During what period of your life have you been the happiest? Explain.

481. What working conditions do you or would you look for when applying for a job? Explain.

482. What are the advantages (or disadvantages) of young children's going to day-care centers instead of staying home? Discuss.

483. Which college courses were most difficult for you? Discuss.

484. How is your generation different from your parents' generation? Discuss.

485. Should couples in the United States be discouraged from having more than two children? Discuss.

486. If your need for sleep were reduced to only one or two hours, what would you do with the added time while others are sleeping?

487. What kinds of people do you enjoy most? Explain.

488. Do you have the skills to run a private business? Explain.

489. What things about yourself would you most like to improve? Explain.

490. Have your attitudes changed much in the last five years? Explain.

491. If you suddenly found that your home was on fire and you had time to rescue only a few belongings, what would you save? Explain.

492. Do you watch talk shows on television? Why or why not?

493. Do you listen to radio talk shows? Why or why not?